KATIE SCHNACK

Everything Is (NOT) Fine

FINDING STRENGTH WHEN LIFE
GETS ANNOYINGLY DIFFICULT

An imprint of InterVarsity Press
Downers Grove, Illinois

InterVarsity Press
P.O. Box 1400 | Downers Grove, IL 60515-1426
ivpress.com | email@ivpress.com

©2023 by Katie Schnack, LLC

InterVarsity Press® is the publishing division of InterVarsity Christian Fellowship/USA®. For more information, visit intervarsity.org.

While any stories in this book are true, some names and identifying information may have been changed to protect the privacy of individuals.

Published in association with Books & Such Literary Management, 2222 Cleveland Avenue #1005, Santa Rosa, CA, 95403, www.booksandsuch.com

The publisher cannot verify the accuracy or functionality of website URLs used in this book beyond the date of publication.

Cover design: David Fassett
Interior design: Daniel van Loon

ISBN 978-1-5140-0614-6 (print) | ISBN 978-1-5140-0615-3 (digital)

Printed in the United States of America ♾

Library of Congress Cataloging-in-Publication Data
Names: Schnack, Katelyn Marie, 1987- author.
Title: Everything is (not) fine : finding strength when life gets annoyingly difficult / Katie Schnack.
Description: Downers Grove, IL : IVP, [2023]	Includes bibliographical references.
Identifiers: LCCN 2023011275 (print)	LCCN 2023011276 (ebook)	ISBN 9781514006146 (print)	ISBN 9781514006153 (digigital)
Subjects: LCSH: Christian women–Religious life.	Suffering–Religious aspects–Christianity.	Resilience (Personality trait)
Classification: LCC BV4527 .S276 2023 (print)	LCC BV4527 (ebook)	DDC 248.8/6–dc23/eng/20230530
LC record available at https://lccn.loc.gov/2023011275
LC ebook record available at https://lccn.loc.gov/2023011276

30   29   28   27   26   25   24   23 | 12   11   10   9   8   7   6   5   4   3   2   1

To Kyle, Sunny, and Shepherd

Contents

You are stronger than you realize. And so is God.

Have you ever found yourself in a situation that really sucked, but you had to keep walking through it anyway? Cool, me too. This book is going to talk about times like that. And other stuff that isn't so depressing, like being strong and kicking life's butt like a vintage Rocky Balboa in his best moment. Because with seasons of hard come seasons of conquering. It isn't all just doom and gloom, even though it may feel that way for some time.

There was one time of my life where this was very clearly the theme—things were really difficult and not fun, but I had to do them anyway. Even though everything in my mind and body would have preferred to hide in my bed for a concerning amount of time and numb my feelings by zoning out on a never-ending TikTok scroll.

My son, Shepherd, was born with medical complexities. A solid handful of them, on very important parts like heart, spinal cord, spine, and kidneys, darn it. It began by identifying he had a heart defect in the womb. Eventually, we would discover the rest. Come to find out, he has a rare condition called VACTERL. It is an acronym for vertebral defects, anal atresia, cardiac defects, tracheo-esophageal fistula, renal anomalies, and limb abnormalities. I bet you were not expecting to see the word *anal* so soon in this book, but here we are. Life sometimes throws curveballs. VACTERL occurs in about 1 in 10,000–40,000 births a year.[1] This means there's approximately a 0.004 percent chance your child will have VACTERL.[2] What are the statistics on winning the lottery again? Should I go buy a Powerball ticket?

When Shepherd was only six months old, still a sweet, squishy, drooling bundle of joy, we had to get a sedated MRI so we could fully identify all of his body's differences and decide a care plan for him. No parent should ever have to walk into a children's hospital and hand their tiny, precious, fragile child over to an anesthesiologist and just "hope and pray for the best" they bring him back to you.

But of course, it didn't end there. At the time, that first MRI and handing him over to a nurse was the hardest moment of my life. But what would follow would be a string of others, each one equally as painful on my mom heart. Tests and diagnosis and months of worry and waiting. More MRIs, more anesthesia, a really weird test where they had to inject him with radiation, and then, surgery. It was all more than a lot.

After that very first MRI, we were scheduled for another one about a year later to see how things had progressed and try to further identify treatment options. This meant we would go back to the same hospital and do it all over. We would again hand over our precious boy to a team of strangers, watch as they wheeled him into a room alone, and sit, wait, and worry,

----

[1] "VATER Syndrome/VACTERL Association," Cincinnati Children's, updated March 2020, www.cincinnatichildrens.org/health/v/vacterl.
[2] Dang, I just did the most math I have done in years.

separated from him for the next three hours. Because reliving trauma is so fun.

As you can imagine, I did not want to do the MRI again. One big ol' bout of parental medical trauma was enough for me, thank you very much. But it wasn't my choice. Life doesn't always play out exactly like we would plan for ourselves—I know you know. We had to yet again walk through the very hard scary thing, even though everything in my body was screaming NO THANK YOU. HARD PASS. I'd rather just be at home nursing and snuggling my son, feeding him puffs and making him laugh and watching him as he sleeps on his own accord, not sedated and hooked up to a million machines with who-knows-what pumping through him.

For two weeks leading up to the MRI, it was all I could think about. I felt like my heartbeat was solely fueled by anxiety, and it was really wearing me down.

Having to fully trust in God when it comes to your kids, with something you love more than life itself, can be hard. A true test of faith. Yes, I fully believe God is good and is with us at every step, but also, that doesn't guarantee outcomes . . . so yeah. That is not an easy little tidbit to accept. And sometimes, it even scares me—the lack of control we have. I think it is okay to admit that even though we trust the Lord, it can sometimes be hard to not be horrified about what is going to happen when facing big, scary things.

A few days before the second MRI, I was texting with my friend Kelsey. I said to her how I wished I were stronger. I wished I could be more of a "pillar of faith"—an example of a strong, brave parent—during this moment. I sure didn't feel that way. I felt more like a useless wet blanket of fear and worry, desperately begging everyone in my circle and all the faceless strangers on the internet to pray for Shepherd and us, because that is all I knew to do. Worry and ask for prayer.

And what Kelsey texted back was something I will never forget.

Honestly, I don't think anyone is actually that inspirational until they come out to the other side of the hard things. You are FAITHFUL because you are asking for prayer and running to God for HELP.

We should change what we think it means to be inspirational.

It isn't about doing everything "perfectly," but about being true to yourself. Being honest with the hard feelings. It is like what they say about courage. Courage doesn't mean you are not scared. It means you are scared and do it anyway.

Did you hear that? *We should change what it means to be inspirational.* It isn't about walking through the hard stuff perfectly, posting smiling Instagram pics along the way. *Look, universe! Look how brave and strong I am! I am doing this all on my own because I am THAT amazing! Why are you not as amazing as me? What a sad shame.* Ugh. We don't need that.

Maybe being honest and open and prayerful as you walk through the hard thing is also an example of strength. Admitting you are scared of the thing and doing it anyway, relying fully on God, might be more of the example we all need to see. So then when the next person goes through the hard thing, they don't feel isolated in their pain.

The second MRI went fine. It wasn't fun, as expected, but it went okay. It was hard, but we made it. I decompressed and fully felt my big sad feelings for a day or so after, then picked back up and kept moving forward.

But guess what, dude? A few more years later, after more specialists and tests and follow-ups, the sedated MRI would look like a cakewalk. And I really love cake, so that says a lot. Eventually, we would realize my son would need spinal cord surgery. Oh gosh. Of all the body parts to operate on! Anything else besides the core of nerves running through his cute little body, please. Couldn't he have needed toe surgery? Perhaps a small mole removed? But even then, I feel it would be just as hard to walk through. Parenting, I tell ya—such a wild ride. We just love these little beasts so much, our heart beats for them.

We had thought we had more time before the surgery—a year maybe. But after a meeting with his neurosurgeon and discussing some onset symptoms we had noticed, she urged us to get it done immediately. At that very same time, I was working on finishing up this book. So now, as I was writing about doing hard things, I was walking through the very hardest thing I have had to experience to date. The irony of life.

Suddenly, I had to think about everything I wrote in these pages. Did it *really* stand up when facing tough times? Was I holding back, or being brutally honest? Was I downplaying pain?

As I made my final edits, I ran everything through this test: If someone said the things I said in this book to me now, as I was really, really struggling, would I want to give them a hug or judo chop them in the throat?

With the surgery looming, I was forced to measure the words in this book against that scale. Everything was being held to the fire. Which is a good thing! But goodness I wish it could have been done in a less dramatic fashion.

So just know that when I finished writing this book, I was in one of the most emotionally challenging places I have ever been in. No fake toxic positivity will be found within these pages—we ain't got time for that, Susan. Just raw honesty and a perspective from someone who was walking through one of the hardest things she has ever had to face.

But what about you? What long, difficult thing are you facing? A hard patch of your marriage? A stressful job with a boss you swear is Medusa herself? A sick child, loneliness, flat-out grief? A pandemic? Whatever it is or was, I hope this book helps you feel less alone with your big feelings, your questions, your hurt. And also, I hope it gently encourages you to keep your eyes on hope.

I think when we walk through extra hard seasons, we can look back and see, in most cases, how our inner strength and God's strength rose up from some miraculous place and got us through. One way or the other, we got through. I know for me, as I write this, the only thing keeping me from having a complete nuclear emotional meltdown is prayer and God's grace. Because on paper, I should be a mess. And some (most) days I am. But somehow, I am getting through, minute by minute, moment by moment, sometimes even with little bits of stolen joy. Little bits of worship music on repeat, snuggles with my kids, and laughing with my husband in our kitchen after bedtime. Just Jesus, honestly, is getting me through in most moments.

Being strong doesn't always look like shouting from the rooftops about how brave and put together we are. For me right now, being strong looks like being honest with my struggles and feelings, asking for prayer, and then expecting peace to show up like God promises. Peace that surpasses my understanding. Because sometimes, that is all we can manage.

Perhaps, being honest and vulnerable and fully leaning on God to get us through is one of the strongest things we can do.

Difficult seasons come, but they also go. I like that part best. I do believe joy is often just around the corner. Good things are also possible, and it is so important we don't forget that, even when we are in the darkest part of the valley.

Guys. God is strong enough to carry us through the times that seem impossible. He not only just carries us like a sad sack of potatoes on his shoulders, but even helps us walk upright in the midst of them. I know, because that is how I am at this exact moment, as I write this sentence. I am standing by the grace of God. A bit wobbly but standing. I might *look* like a sack of potatoes, but that is to be expected under such dire circumstances, so we will let that slide for now.

As I look back at the first few years of my son's life, filled with specialists and hospital trips and pokes and tests—I can see how God carried us, during every twist, turn, and bump in the road. I can see that God not only did get us through, but sometimes he even brought tiny bits of joy, even on the scariest days. A miracle. I can see how I can stand a little bit stronger on my own two feet now, because of what we walked through. And as I keep pressing on, I know he will do just the same, again and again.

And I do believe that he will do the same for you. I really, really do. I do believe he can carry you through whatever hard thing it is you have to face. He will give you peace, and give you strength. And, I do think you might be surprised at your own strength along the way too, you little baddie.

Hard stuff is, well, hard. It definitely isn't fun. But it is making you stronger. You might not appreciate that now, but you will one day, I know it.

We can keep our eyes on hope. We can remember that God is stronger than we realize. And you are stronger than you realize too.

PART 1

Don't make it a thing until it's a thing.

WORRYING IS PAYING INTEREST ON A
DEBT YOU MIGHT NOT EVEN OWE.
....
Mark Twain . . . maybe. Google is vague about who
actually said this first, but it's still a great quote.

I HAVE AN AMAZING AUNT Sue who gave birth to
two-pound premature twn girls back in the eighties.
Having preemie twins in today's time with today's
amazing technology advancements is scary in itself.
I can't even imagine what it was like when most of the
world still thought tight perms and ratted-out bangs
were a good idea.

After I became a mom myself, I finally fully realized
how stressful that whole process must have been, and
I asked her about it. I couldn't even imagine having
babies so small, so fragile. She told me after her girls
were born, there were countless worries and fears
swirling around them, at every point. Endless thoughts
of *What if this happens?* as every real, scary, and

possible scenario was presented to them. But, for mental survival purposes, she and my Uncle Randy adopted the mantra of "Don't make it a thing until it's a thing."

Years later, I was walking through the medical stuff with Shepherd, when we were so in the dark about what his diagnosis would be, if his heart would be strong enough to keep pumping, or if his special back bones and tethered spinal cord would allow him to grow and thrive and walk, and she reminded me: *Don't make it a thing until it's a thing.*

And it was exactly what I needed to hear, from someone who had also walked through the scary dark parts of having medically complex children and come out on the other side.

Until you *actually* get the news, until you *actually* get the test results, don't make it a thing until it is a thing.

Until you actually have that meeting with your boss, actually have the uncomfortable boundary-setting conversation with your family, or whatever thing looming in front of you that seems big and scary, don't make it a "thing" until, well, it is. Because it could all be *nothing*. Not as big and scary and awful as our minds had told us it would be. Sometimes things do turn out fine.

And I bet you know that, at some level. I know that, even though sometimes it is easy to forget. So let's keep reminding ourselves about that, gently. Let's not make it a thing until it is a thing.

Okay—but now can I tell you about the time I almost got eaten by a grizzly bear? Because that was actually . . . a thing.

CHAPTER ONE

Keep your eyes on the path and don't step in bear poop.

I like to hike in the mountains, but I also have anxiety. Sometimes those things don't work well together.

When my husband, Kyle, and I were nineteen, we spent an entire summer living and working in Glacier National Park, Montana. We lived in a little white cabin built in the 1930s at Swiftcurrent Motor Inn with a bunch of other roommates and a communal bathroom with concrete showers. Everyone there that summer, just like decades of employees that came before us, was there to do two things: work a little and hike a lot. The resort sat right in the heart of a valley surrounded by mountains, with endless trails to hike, mountains to summit, and backcountry campgrounds to explore. The lakes in Glacier are teal, the mountains have snow on them, and at any point you can run into a mountain goat, which is pretty awesome.

Kyle and I would crank out twelve-hour double shifts at the restaurant, doling out trail recommendations and bear-avoidance advice to the tourists dining at our tables between their soda refills. We would tell them what hikes were closed because of bear activity, what hikes were easy, what ones were hard, what ones were the most beautiful. If we really liked the tourists, we would tell them about the secret lake where a handful of massive moose would gather each night to eat, but mostly that was sacred insider knowledge.

Then, after two days of double shifts spent smiling, chatting, and serving, we would head into the wilderness. We would hike our favorite trails and try our hand at off-trail climbing, armed with nothing but a book written in the 1970s that vaguely explained where to go. We would do backcountry camping trips way up in the mountains, cuddling a can of bear spray the entire night, just in case. We would hike and hike until our socks were bloody on the heels and our legs felt like al dente noodles. It was magic. That summer, Kyle and I both logged more than 250 miles and loved every second of it.

The reason we knew about Glacier to begin with is because my own father worked there in college, and then took us out almost every summer of my childhood. The first time I summited a mountain was as a one-year-old in a sketchy 1980s baby-carrying hiking backpack with a metal frame. My family went back for years after that on family vacations. So as Kyle and I drove away from such an idyllic summer that year to return to college, we knew we would be back to the park.

And we did return, a few years later with my mom, dad, sister, and brother-in-law. Kyle and I were in our midtwenties then, freshly married and neck deep in Kyle's grad school program. Our brains, at the ripe age of twenty-five, had finally fully developed. Or at least that's what my mom told me. She'd frequently remind me, "Remember your brain isn't fully developed yet!" anytime I wanted to do something stupid from the ages of eighteen to twenty-four. She is definitely not a doctor, but things moms say always feel real.

Even though we were not super youthful anymore, and our frontal lobes were now plump and fully cooked, we still kinda *felt* like we were young. Feeling like an old person usually kicks in around thirty-three. So on that trip, Kyle and I wanted to do a really big hike, just like we did back in our glory days. I mean, those times of hiking triumph were only a handful of years prior—we could still do it, right? A short few years of stress, studying, drinking cheap beer out late with friends, and shame eating Taco Bell in our cars alone one-too-many times surely had no effect on our physical ability, right? We were twenty-five! Practically invincible!

We decided to hike the Highline, which is a seven-mile trail set at about seven thousand feet above sea level and one of our all-time favorites. Some parts of the trail are so narrow and high on the side of a cliff that there is a garden hose nailed right into rock so you can hang on and not, well, fall off and die. I am fairly sure it is the same hose my dad clung to with me in the baby backpack. It is always fun having your entire existence on earth dependent on cracked vintage rubber and old nails, right?

But the meager Highline wasn't enough for us—that is for the common tourist humans. We were Glacier regulars after all. We knew the tricks and secrets and wanted to go all out.

So, we walked the seven-mile trail overlooking deep mountain valleys and bright teal lakes so beautiful they didn't seem real. We stepped over small patches of snow that crossed in front of us, saw some cute goats, and filled up our water bottles in ice-cold streams trickling down the mountain. At the end of the trail was a little chalet, where we stopped, ate a candy bar, drank a Gatorade, and continued on our way.

Most people at this point simply turn around and hike back, or take a little loop trail straight down through the woods and catch a shuttle that takes you back to the trailhead parking lot. But we wanted to keep going. If we continued on a bit, we could do a one-mile climb almost straight up to a fire lookout where a ranger lived—how intriguing! So we did. But the ranger wasn't even there—what prior engagement they had that particular afternoon is beyond me. Perhaps there was a sale going on at IKEA two states over and they casually stepped away.

So there Kyle and I sat at the top of the mountain and tried to catch our breath. We had run out of water—the cold, lovely streams were now a far thing of the past, so, in desperation, we drank the juice from fruit cups we had packed. As we sat there, high on the mountain, we looked down—way down—into the valley where our cabins were. That is where we were heading. Easy, right? False.

We were already exhausted and had hiked ten miles and gained thousands of feet in elevation. Now, we had to basically do it all over again, but on a downward angle.

Oh. And it was starting to get dark out—the shady subtle stillness that comes right before dusk. The shadows were getting longer, the air just a bit breezier and cooler. We knew not only were we going to have to make it down the gigantic cliff, but we were going to have to hustle.

I think at this point we finally realized we most definitely were not nineteen anymore. The sheer optimism of our fully developed brains was not enough to keep us going full steam. We were exhausted and winded and our legs felt weak, like little potbelly pigs with asthma. At this point, I began to question all of the day's prior choices leading us to the top of this very tall mountain, miles away from the comfort of our cabin and ample supply of snacks. What was the point in all this again?

But there was only one option. To keep going forward even though we didn't want to. The situation didn't feel great. We were not feeling great. But we had to keep walking forward even though it was hard.

So, Kyle and I ate the sad remaining soggy fruit from our cups, picked ourselves up, and began to hike the mile back down the lookout mountain. As we began walking the short trail toward the cliff, we were surprised to see a group of hikers on their way up the valley. It was getting late in the day, and this wasn't a popular trail, so we were not expecting to see anyone.

We gave little winded half waves to the group as we approached, and one said to us, between pants of breath and with worried wrinkles on their forehead, "You are not going down that way, are you?" pointing to the trail we were about to descend.

Kyle and I looked at each other. Why were they asking that? *Yes. Yes, winded concerned human. That is where we are going.*

We had no other choice! This group walking up was staying at the chalet—something you have to book a year in advance. There was no room at the inn for us there. And we couldn't hike back where we came from—we would never make it eight miles before it was pitch black and we were left groping in the dark for the stupid garden hose nailed into the cliff. We couldn't go down the loop at this point—the shuttle had stopped running, we had no car, and there was no cell phone service to call someone to pick us up. And while we did hitchhike a bit in our youthful days in Glacier . . . NOPE. That chapter had long passed. So yes, we were going down that trail, because we had to.

"Yeah, our cabins are down in the valley," Kyle explained.

"Well, there is a huge grizzly bear on the trail," they said. "Be careful."

Cool cool cool guys, cool cool. So now not only was it getting dark and we were exhausted with miles left to go, but there was also a furry death beast in our direct vicinity that could jump out at any moment and devour us like we were nothing more than a blood-filled Pop-Tart.

We got to the top of the cliff and looked ahead at the switchback path, which had to zigzag one way, then cut back sharply the other because of how steep the mountainside was. This section of the trail, since not as frequented by tourists, did not come with a garden hose on the wall. But oh, how I wish it did. Because apparently, since our brains were now "fully developed," we were now able to realize just how terrifying this narrow trail really was. When we did it years before, I didn't think twice about it. Now, I was horrified. One stumble or step on loose rock and well, ya know. Falling, certain death, and all that jazz. So lame.

And oh yeah, the grizzly bear was also a very real issue.

But again, we had to keep moving forward. We had to walk down the narrow, scary path with the potential of encountering a teddy bear from hell, all before it got pitch black outside and our family called the rangers for a dramatic search-and-rescue situation.

We in no way wanted to, but we *had* to keep going. Did we feel strong enough? That was questionable. Did we feel emotionally calm, brave, and ready to tackle it? Not a chance—we were terrified. But somehow, we still had to walk forward.

So, we began the descent. My heart was pounding, my breaths were shallow, and everything around me felt fuzzy and spinny.

My anxiety—which I sometimes get just walking in grocery stores on solid ground—was at peak levels as I tried not to look down over the cliff ledge. Kyle was also visibly nervous, which says a lot. The man is usually a stoic, so if he expresses one tiny feeling, it means he is feeling it times one hundred.

We, two scared and exhausted twenty-five-year-olds, began a little chant. A rhythm that kept us going ahead, focusing on exactly what was in front of us, not the big frightening situation surrounding us. Like total hiking dorks, we started to say together out loud, "Right foot, left foot. Right foot, left foot." Over and over we repeated that, watching exactly where each foot fell on the path and keeping our eyes firmly fixed on what we could control.

With fear swirling around us, we had to simplify and focus in. Right foot, left foot was all we could muster in that moment. "Right foot, left foot" was the chant and mantra keeping us moving forward. By focusing on what was exactly in front of us, not all the possibility for doom and destruction surrounding us, we were able to remain (mostly) calm, and just take the next step we knew to take. Then the next, on whatever solid ground we could see in front of us. They were not fancy steps, big steps, or fast steps, but we kept doing them. Little by little, bit by bit, making our way through the super hard stuff, until the walk was safer, easier.

But it wasn't just the fear of falling down the massive cliff that was throwing us off. As we were walking, even while being careful and taking little steps, something else got in our way. Fresh, steaming piles of grizzly bear poop. That group of hikers was right to express their concern. There was a big ol' bear in our midst, as evidenced by these stanky half-digested berry piles still warm to the touch.[1]

---

[1] Okay wait—to be clear, I didn't actually touch the poop piles. You could just feel they were warm from their glisten and swarming flies. Ew.

But guess what—we didn't let the unwanted poop piles distract us from our focus on the path ahead. Right foot, left foot, step over the extra piles of crap trying to throw us off, and keep moving forward to the end game. We couldn't control if there was a bear. We could only control the steps we took to move forward, so that is where we focused.

Finally, we made it down into the tree line where things felt less steep, and then to flat, safe, solid ground. Well, mostly safe. Yes, we were not at risk of falling, but we still had miles of trail through the woods as the sky got darker by the minute, with the very real possibility of a grizzly showing up around any corner. The moment we hit flat ground, we knew what we had to do: run. So, we ran the rest of the way back, fueled by adrenaline and the very real fear that we could be eaten by a furry, wild beast, our bodies suddenly forgetting we had just hiked more than a dozen miles. So we ran and ran, no more talking, no more right foot left foot, just our entire bodies and minds focused on finishing the hike and getting to a better spot. By the grace of God, the bear's fresh poop was as much of him as we encountered. We didn't even hear a grunt from the brush or an ominous rustle in the bushes. Whatever he was after that night, it wasn't us.

But then after about a mile of our desperate sprint through the woods toward the finish line, I heard something. Someone was calling out a whistle, loud and repetitive. It was my dad, somewhere further down the trail from us, making the sound of a loon call. It was the same sound we hear every summer night at our cabin in the north woods of Minnesota, and also the whistle that we make when we are lost in Target and need to find each other. It is very helpful, this familiar family whistle, but expect to get a few weird looks from people if you try it when you get lost in the hypnotic haze of Studio McGee pillows. But there in the woods that evening, my dad had started doing the hike in reverse to look for us, knowing it was getting concerningly dark and we were still somewhere out in the vast wilderness. It was basically a mountain rescue, on a very small and nondramatic scale.

I can still hear the sound of his whistle, and remember the spark of joy and relief it put in my heart as it cut through the now mostly dark woods. I knew we were done, and it was going to be okay. No, my dad couldn't be there as we took step by step over piles of bear poop. He couldn't physically carry our aging bodies up and down the thousands of feet of elevation. Mostly because he is way more aged himself, clearly. At this point it would be far more likely for us to be carrying him around. Kyle and I had to do the hard work of the hike ourselves. We had to take the emotional steps forward on our own.

But my dad was thinking of us the entire time we were gone. And then, he was there to meet us at the end. Kinda like God cares about us and thinks about us and loves us when we are walking through our own hard seasons, on our own scary trails full of poop and unknown. Except God actually is right there with us, the entire time, helping us along. We might not see him every step of the way. We may need to step over the piles of bear crap on our own, but he is with us to strengthen us, protect us, and guide us down the best path.

So, Kyle, my dad, and I tackled the last mile of the trail together, as the dusk began to settle in and the crickets got louder. When we got to the little circle of white vintage cabins we were all staying in, Kyle and I collapsed in camping chairs and washed away our adrenaline and anxieties with food, drinks, and a dramatic retelling of our day to my family. This, to me, is the very best part of big scary outdoor adventures—retelling the story.

I will always remember the little focused rhythm Kyle and I had to get into in order not to, well, freak out. Right foot, left foot, again and again. All you can do is just keep taking the next step ahead of you that you know to take. Avoid the piles of crap that show up in your path that will try and throw you off, and keep going forward, little by little until you reach a more solid ground. Right foot, left foot, eyes focused on the next little step to take.

Have you ever been through something like that? Not necessarily a crazy hike, but in life? Having to walk through something really hard and frankly scary that you did not want to walk through, but had no other option—boo. A breakup. A death. The dumb pandemic. An illness. A sick child. A rocky marriage. Ya know—all those tough, complicated things. We all go through these at some point, right?

That wild hike—which included a rogue grizzly bear because why not—taught me two things about hard seasons. First, you can push yourself farther than you think you can go, especially if that is the only option. You *are* stronger than you realize, and sometimes you have to be forced a bit to see that side of you. I wish this never happened to anybody. I wish the only thing we were forced to do was take a nap with a gaggle of kittens. But sometimes, life pushes us to do things that stretch us physically, emotionally, even spiritually, and in those moments, we *can* grow.

Second, narrowing your focus to what is exactly in front of you, exactly what you can control, is vital for survival. For the hike, it was the exact next step to take that was safe, right in front of me. Not fixing your eyes on the dizzying, scary things surrounding you, but the solid little bit of ground you know to be safe. And then the next. Keep moving forward, even if your steps are slow and shaky.

In times like these, I hope you know that God is there, cheering for you and loving you fiercely. He can provide you strength as you stumble along the path. Even if you don't fully feel or see him at the time, he is *always* there and will see you through. And, by his grace there will be an end to the hard passage. The grizzly bear eventually takes a nap in a cave. The path gets easier—less of a life-and-death situation and more solid flat ground. One day, this long hard thing may even end, and there might be a chance to rest and reflect. Perhaps, if we are so lucky, the hard things will even become a good story to tell. Or at least something to remember and keep tucked in your heart as you keep on walking forward, step by step.

CHAPTER TWO

....

Listen to your kid's singing, even if it is obnoxious.

Kids can teach us a lot of things. Even if they are not our own! A niece, a nephew, a friend's baby, or a cute little squishy beast in the grocery store waving at you like you are their new best friend can still bring us life insights. Their simplicity, love, and imagination can help us see past our narrow adult way of thinking to something a bit bigger, more magical. We need reminders like that sometimes. Kids teach us things like the true meaning of unconditional love and how we all need so much grace, each and every day. They teach us to slow down and find joy in the small things in life—that we don't need much to be happy. They teach us how to be adaptable and what is truly important. They teach us there is always space to be had for jokes, play, and dancing like a fool, just by being their sweet, wild selves.

But have you ever had God use your child's annoying singing to bop you over the head with some divine truth?[1]

....

[1]Sorry, Sunny of the future reading this, that I called your singing annoying. I mean, most times I love it and would prefer it to an entire Beyoncé performance, but sometimes . . . shh. Just . . . shh.

The first year of Shepherd's life, our thoughts and lives were vastly consumed by the visits to the children's hospital, finding new specialists and second opinions, scary tests, waiting on the results of the scary tests, and a general sense of worry and dread about what was to come for our child.

There was nothing I could do to fix our situation or get us out of it. Kyle and I were coming to realize caring for Shepherd's special needs was a marathon—possibly an unending one. There were no answers or solutions, but a constant monitoring of multiple different issues, and simply hoping and praying that things behaved and got better as he grew older.

It was a lot to adjust to—the realization that there was no clear light at the end of this tunnel. Honestly, a new tunnel could pop up at any moment, really. And because of that, we were forced to live within this never-ending vortex of worry and fear and what-ifs, without any tangible way to get off the ride. And granted this was a ride I was pretty sure I wasn't even qualified to be on in the first place—riders must have at least forty-eight inches of spiritual and emotional strength to board. I felt I had a solid twelve on a good day.

As we navigated our new reality as parents to a very medically complex child, there would be so many nights I would be lying in bed staring at the ceiling at three in the morning, my heart physically feeling squeezed from anxiety. Not knowing what the next day, the next appointment, and the general future would hold for my sweet boy was emotionally taxing and consumed most of my thoughts. Especially the thoughts that popped up in the middle of the night, darn it.

Have you ever had nights like that? When you are wide awake yet exhausted all at the same time? Maybe you are not even staring at the ceiling because your eyes are squeezed shut in pain or blurred with tears that just keep falling. Have you ever laid there, dreading the sun coming up because that means you will have to go face the scary thing, hear the potentially bad news, or even just get up and do the whole melancholy, depressed drudge of the day all over again like a boring version of the movie *Groundhog Day* that doesn't even include a cute furry creature?

Those nights are so hard. I would prefer a bad nightmare that I could wake up from to those sleepless nights when your mind is swirling around a nightmare that is actually real. Right after the discovery of Shepherd's heart defect—the very first sign something was off with him—I would wake up in the middle of the night and think, *Dang, what a bad dream*, before realizing it wasn't a dream, but it was our real-life situation. I wish that nights like that would never happen, to you, to me, to anyone.

One of those restless nights, I was lying in bed, trying not to think about the weight of the things ahead of us. Potential surgeries, if my son would ever be able to walk, if his heart defect was going to cause him to, well . . . die . . . All the really fun things that I apparently had on my plate were just on an unending loop, and I was so, so over it. Out of desperation, I began repeating the Bible verse "Let the morning bring me word of your unfailing love, for I have put my trust in you."[2] Over and over and over I would repeat that verse, praying it, hoping for it, begging God to just help me feel better tomorrow, if nothing else. To help me have a better day—one where I feel peace instead of fear, strength instead of defeat.

[2]Psalm 143:8. Serious footnotes are few and far between in my writing so enjoy this normalcy for a moment.

I really needed his help at that moment because without it, I didn't see how I could get my butt out of bed the next day. How beneath the emotional weight I was feeling, I could also parent, work, function as a human being even. It seemed impossible all on my own. So I was trying so hard to just put all my trust in the simple promises of God, because there wasn't much else keeping my boat afloat at that time. In fact, it felt like every little thing was just trying to sink it further into the deepest part of the ocean. So deep, there were random alien-looking fish creatures without dangling flashlights coming out of their forehead. That is how deep I felt. Scary deep. Weird deep. Impossibly deep to emerge from unscathed.

So I prayed: *Lord Jesus, let the morning bring me word of your unfailing love, for I have put my trust in you. Let the morning bring me word of your unfailing love, for I have put my trust in you.* Rinse and repeat, a million times, until at last I fell asleep. A tired mom's desperate plea in the night for a brighter day tomorrow, for her babies, for her family. For all of the things.

The next morning, I woke up to begin the rhythm of all that is ordinary in the life of a parent of a baby and a toddler. After drinking as much iced coffee as possible without my head combusting, I dove into the morning chaos in all its glory. I was rushing around the house, trying to get some sort of acceptable clothing on myself and my tiny humans. I was making school lunches and bagging up snacks and hunting down milk bottles and water bottles that always seem to be stolen and hidden by some sort of mysterious beverage container–snatching troll. My mind was so focused on all the mundane yet oh-so-important tasks I had to complete before we could get out the door for daycare and get started on work. Upstairs, downstairs, into the laundry room, diving headfirst and swimming deep into the dirty laundry pile to find one more clean baby sock—all the things.

As I was doing that, my precious four-year-old, Sunny, started doing something weird. Kids are by far the oddest of creatures in all the land. Most times they do really cute, average stuff, like saying words in a silly way or gracing you with the best giggles of all time. But sometimes they go rogue. And you just look at them like—*what? Why and how? Why would you use your dirty underwear to make a nest for your dinosaur egg and then surround it with tiny toy bears and a fake marshmallow?* Sometimes they just make no sense. This day, in the thick of the morning rush, Sunny began following me around the house like we were tied together by some sort of invisible cord. She was at my heels, would not give me more than three inches of space, and she was singing. Loudly. Like nonstop, put the track on repeat, and then drop-your-phone-into-the-car-seat-crack-while-driving-on-the-highway level of repeat.

Oh, my lovely little cute lady, how I love your singing . . . in any other time but now. Can't you see I have THINGS to DO? All these dumb, important THINGS must take precedence over your musical performance. Those are the inner thoughts of every busy mom, right? Or just me? Feel free to email me and let me know that I am a terrible mother if you want.[3]

Anyway, Sunny was trailing me around and singing at the top of her lungs, the same few lines, over and over again. I was half tuning her out, my mind so focused on just trying to get out the door, when I stopped abruptly. So much so, she almost crashed headfirst into my butt.

---

[3]But actually don't.

I stopped, because for a split second I finally took my brain out of the whirlwind of all that needed to be done, and it actually heard exactly *what* she was singing. And, believe it or not, it wasn't the soundtrack to *Moana*, which at that time she would watch daily. It was "Jesus Loves Me."

Jesus loves me this I know,
for the Bible tells me so . . .
Jesus loves me this I know,
for the Bible tells me so.

Apparently, that is the only part of the song she knew, so she sang it over, and over, and over, like a skipping CD in a cheap 1990s boombox.

It finally clicked for me, and I started laughing. Just a few hours before, as I lay in bed full of worry, I had begged God to let the morning bring me word of his unfailing love. *Please God, let the morning bring me word of your unfailing love.*

And now, there was a tiny creature trailing me around the house, loudly yelling about God's love for me, over and over. Dang.

Two things felt very clear to me at this moment.

First, God hears me. I knew that of course, but to see such a direct answer will never not feel amazing. Because it doesn't always happen that way. But sometimes, it does. And it is beautiful. He hears you too, by the way. I know that as well. And, if you want to borrow my daughter for a very tangible reminder of that, she is now booking answer-to-prayer singing telegrams via Cameo.

Second, it showed me that God has a sense of humor. And everyone can appreciate a good sense of humor, right? Especially divine ones. Because guys, I was in a dark, sad spot. I was lying in my bed on unwashed, questionably smelling sheets with dirty, frizzy hair and tear-stained cheeks, begging God to just do something—anything—to get me through the next day. That is all I had the strength to even ask for. It felt like there was nothing to look forward to except another day of worrying about Shepherd, mixed with a side of work, toddler meltdowns, and that pesky giant pile of dishes in the sink that continued to refuse to put themselves into the dishwasher.

But, that morning was a brand-new day. And in that moment, God made me laugh, reminded me that he hears me and that he cares about me. He used my curly-haired, wild daughter and her loud confident singing voice to tangibly show his love for me—the exact thing I had been praying for the night prior.

Sometimes, God showing his love for us doesn't show up as obviously as this instance. It can be more subtle. Sometimes it comes slowly, quietly, unassuming. Maybe it shows up in a perfect cup of coffee in the morning and a moment to breathe, or with the gift of an extra bougie sunrise. With the gift of friendships and laughing until tears flow. Perhaps we just need to open our eyes, or in my case, ears, to really see it, feel it, envelop it, and experience it.

There of course came more nights where there was more worry than sleep. More nights where I would repeat Scripture to try and calm my clenched heart so I could get some rest. Where I begged God to make things change, make things feel easier, show me his mercy and love the next morning. While after those nights, Sunny didn't magically come in and follow me around singing exactly what I needed to hear, I did remember the time she did, and that was enough. I remembered that, and every other tiny time that God moved and worked and showed up, and I knew God was still there. I knew he was still going to walk with me through the day, and whatever it held, both good and bad. And I believe he will do the same for you too. If you are having a night that seems impossible, or a day . . . or a week, whatever—I pray you, too, will remember to ask him to draw close, provide you peace if there is no tangible way to fix whatever it is your heart is aching about, and ask to feel his love with each new morning.[4]

[4]Begging works also.

CHAPTER THREE

....

It might not get easier. Sorry.
But! You can get used to it.

Some things in life are so awful they won't ever be "okay."

How is that for an encouraging way to start a chapter? *Cue the doom and gloom music worthy of the Addams Family mansion.*

But there is a little bit of good news in this, so take heart!

Whatever hard thing you are facing—the death of someone you love, a sick child, living far away from the love of your life, or having a dog with persistent stinky butt glands—it might not ever be "okay." But! You can get used to it.[1]

That is good, right? But I can't take credit. A random internet friend whose son also has VACTERL said it, and I will never forget it.[2] Let's discuss.

For the first two years of Shepherd's life, we didn't know he had VACTERL. When he was in utero, we learned he had a

....

[1]Except the gland thing. That will never be okay.

[2]Not only did our sons have the same rare condition, but we also both came from Minnesota and had pet goats. WHAT ARE THE ODDS? Note: the goats came *after* Shepherd was born, so one can conclude that owning goats does not cause your child to be born with VACTERL. I am basically a doctor at this point considering the way I can put two and two together.

heart defect so that was the main focus of our doctor visits and anxieties for a while. But then, when he began sitting up, we realized he was extremely crooked, that poor little chap. So, we took him in to see a pediatric orthopedic specialist, who took an x-ray of his back, and then quickly rattled off a number of spinal malformations to us, along with the fact he probably had a tethered spinal cord and likely kidney defects as well. The doctor ordered us to get an MRI at the hospital, see a pediatric neurosurgeon, a urologist, an orthopedic surgeon, and a geneticist.

Kyle and I went in thinking the doctor would likely recommend some physical therapy to help straighten Shepherd out, and we left with our entire worlds flipped upside down. My little tiny sweet dude with two sweet teeth poking through his drooly baby gums now required a medical team big enough to successfully fill up one side of a sand volleyball court.

So we spent hours calling and scheduling and booking appointments, and we tried our best to mentally and physically prepare ourselves for the barrage of tests and meetings that we wished we never had to have in the first place.

Eventually, we would find out his genetic test was clear. There was no identifiable gene or known genetic syndrome that caused his malformations. This was great news, on paper! But immediately my mom guilt kicked in to super overdrive. If it wasn't a gene, clearly it was *me* that did this to him, right? Was it that yoga class I took in the first trimester when I didn't realize I was going to be in a heated room? Did I take the wrong kind of prenatal vitamins? Did I not take enough prenatal vitamins? All of these things I now know are not true, but the lies took up a lot of stock in my brain for quite some time, and I know other parents can relate.

Appointment after appointment for each of Shepherd's little special body parts seemed like a long, drawn-out form of parental torture. Of course, we would do anything to make sure that he got the best care. But what that meant was taking off work; driving two hours to the children's hospital in Miami; putting our little child through awful tests where he was hooked up to tubes, poked, scanned, and just all the things that a baby should never have to experience; and then drive two hours home in a cloud of exhaustion, test-result anxiety, and rush-hour traffic. While we were so grateful for the good care that the Miami hospital provided, it was always a long, hard, stress- and traffic-filled day that left me feeling like a shell of a human at the end of it.

Eventually as word got out to our friends and community about what we were going through with Shepherd, I was invited to be in a private Facebook group called "Warrior Moms" for parents of children with medical needs. Posts were mostly asking for doctor recommendations, asking for advice, and giving the occasional rant about just how freaking hard it is to love and care for someone *so* much, and have to see them go through such hardship. We all could relate on a level we wished we never had to.

One day I was posting about Shepherd in that group, asking about physical therapist recommendations, and I listed off all his sweet little body issues. Someone commented "It sounds like your son has VACTERL." I replied—"Oh, no, his genetic test came back clear; he doesn't have a diagnosis." She explained to me that VACTERL isn't something that shows up in genetics. In fact, so little is known about what causes VACTERL that it isn't even considered a "condition," just an association—a regular grouping of body malformations with no genetic cause, no outside cause, no . . . well, basically they have no idea why it happens. But it happens *enough* to know that there is some reason all these specific body parts get a little wonky in utero, so . . . *shrugging emoji.*

I called Shepherd's geneticist to set up a virtual appointment, simply to ask her one question: Does he have VACTERL? She was like, "yes, he does." I said, "oh interesting, thank you," and we politely wrapped up our call. In my brain, I was screaming, WHY DIDN'T YOU TELL ME THAT TWO YEARS AGO THEN? But being the polite former Midwesterner that I am, I smiled, hung up, then bawled my eyes out. We had a name for it, what we had been battling against and trying to understand, and that was important.

I took the rest of the day off work to cry, go kickboxing, and drown my sorrows in Starbucks because with news like that, ya gotta carve out some time to process and grieve. Or punch something and then overly caffeinate until you don't feel your sorrows so strongly anymore—both methods work.

I guess since VACTERL isn't technically a genetically caused condition, it was a bit out of the things the geneticist focused on, or cared about, or . . . I don't know. And all of Shepherd's other specialists were just focused on *one* body part—heart, kidneys, spine, spinal cord—trying to figure out what was happening with just that part, so they all forgot to mention the symptoms were all connected, and it was called VACTERL association. Maybe they even thought I knew? WELL, I DIDN'T. Sigh. The point is, we now had a diagnosis. Did it change anything? Not how we cared for Shepherd, no. But did it change how I felt in my heart? Yes, 100 percent.

The diagnosis mostly took away my irrational guilt over the heated yoga class I accidentally took. Also, it gave me a way to find a community of others who could relate—other people walking through the exact same thing as we were. And quite simply, that meant finding a Facebook group specifically about VACTERL, joining it, and connecting with others going through the same super rare journey. Are these types of groups the only real benefit of social media? Possibly.

So, I found the group and joined. And as I read the posts, I was blown away by how similar everyone's stories were to ours. I thought that we were just walking through some random, awful, heartbreaking string of medical hardships for who knows what reason. And yes, we were, but also what we were experiencing was *normal*, for people who had VACTERL at least. And that meant a lot to me, to know that. To know that we were not the only ones in the universe going through this chaos, and that in fact what seemed so random and awful was actually quite normal. 'Twas the nature of the VACTERL beast.

But then, I got really weird and internet stalker-y. Who doesn't love a good internet snoop and lurk session, right? I looked on Instagram for people using the VACTERL hashtag. There were not a lot, but there were *some*. I began friending and sliding into the DMs of other moms whose kids had VACTERL, with no shame in my game. *Hey girl hey! What body parts are you stressing over today? Let's chat!* And, in all cases, they were happy to connect. There was a lot of power in talking about our similar experiences and promising to help and encourage each other, as best we could, even if from across the world on a tiny phone screen. Shepherd's diagnosis was such a rare, strange thing, that it felt great to geek out over kidney reflux and spinal cords with other moms who understood.

Remember when I was telling you about my random internet friend? The one with a son who has VACTERL, and who was from Minnesota, and has pet goats? The goats being the most exciting part. Well, her name is Jenny, and we chatted and connected really well. We loved discussing the shared experiences of our sons and our mutual love/hate of goat snuggles—while cute, the cuddling can get painful. I have had far too many hoof-shaped bruises on my legs, as had she.

One day, Jenny posted about her son and their medical journey, and she wrote something that impacted me. It's the thing I shared at the beginning of this chapter, something we can all benefit from hearing, no matter what long, hard things we are facing. After years and years of doctors and surgeries and scares, she said, "This has not gotten easier. But we have gotten used to it."

This really helped bandage up a part of my medical mom heart that still felt so raw. Even remembering that now, it loosens something in my chest. And not just leftover congestion from Covid. Something emotionally.

Because sometimes, in life, things don't get easier. And they never will, dang it. So if we spend all of our energy trying to avoid pain, make the "bad thing" disappear, or just pretend that it is all finneeeeeee when it actually is very much NOT fine, we may never begin to heal and grow.

At some point, it becomes easier and more productive to just accept that this "hard thing" we are facing is just . . . hard. Period. And it isn't going to change into anything else. There is no magical metamorphosis for the situation to grow into a beautiful butterfly and fly into the sunset. But *you* can become the butterfly—growing, changing, flying a bit higher—so let's focus on that instead.[3] Let's focus our energy on accepting, and getting *used* to the hard thing, however that may be. A weight-lifter at the gym can lift their personal record heaviness and feel like their arms are about to fall off. But then they do it again, and again, for weeks, and suddenly it is easier. They have become used to the heaviness. They have become stronger, so they can handle more. The literal amount of weight hasn't changed. It is still big, bulky, heavy, and hard. But they are used to it, and therefore able to conquer it all the easier and stand a bit taller doing so.

Managing Shepherd's medical journey and all the pain and emotions that brings to my mom heart may not get easier. But I am getting used to it. And that is something. In fact, I am even slowly coming to terms that there is a very real reality it might get a bit (a.k.a. a lot) more difficult: when we have to move forward with surgeries, or he grows and can better express pain or express his frustrations about having to spend so much time at hospitals. Right now, he mostly just associates doctor's visits with post-appointment ice cream and full-sized toys from the child life specialists.

It might not get easier, but I can get used to it. I can get used to waiting on hold for an hour listening to the stupid hospital music as I wait to book Shepherd's neurosurgery appointment.[4]

....

[3] This was kinda cheesy, the whole butterfly thing. But also a good analogy, so slap it on a cracker because we are rolling in the cheese.

[4] This summer, I will be giving a live performance of the Nicklaus Children's Hospital scheduling line's on-hold music, since I have it so permanently ingrained in my brain. Tickets on sale now via Ticketmaster.

I can find ways to make the long trek to Miami for his tests and checkups a bit more fun for us all. I can expect my mom heart to break in half, yet again, when I have to dress my baby in a tiny hospital gown and hand him over to a stranger, or hold him down while he cries during tests and try my best to comfort him in an impossibly uncomfortable situation. I can expect the hard to be, well, hard. And not much more than that. And then not be surprised when it is, but rather just use what energy I have to make the best out of the crap situation. Because what other option is there? If I can't change it, maybe I can get used to it.

Have you ever faced something like that? Something that you know, unfortunately, cannot be changed or improved or taken away or magically healed. The death of a loved one. A chronic sickness. A really bad haircut with way-too-short bangs.

I believe in miracles, I do. But I also believe that sometimes the miracle isn't always the "bad thing" being taken away, as much as I wish it was. With deep grief, for example, that isn't even really possible, right? If you have lost someone close, you know that the wound may never fully heal up, and you just learn to live with it open. Perhaps then, the miracle is God-breathed strength that inflates you to keep moving forward. To be able to have joy again after a time when you were not sure that was ever going to be possible. It could even be a little miracle to—gasp and clutch your pearls here, folks—make jokes about the "bad thing." Or is that just me who makes jokes about really serious and awful stuff? Well at least me and about two of my close friends. Humor can be healing, especially once you are safely out of the "too soon to joke about it" zone.

It is a miracle for anyone to feel like they stand a bit firmer in the midst of their category-five hardship, and not only exist, not only thrive, but begin to emulate enough light that they can start to encourage and strengthen others who are not able to stand firm in their own journey quite yet.

I pray, I hope, that you don't ever have to walk through something that seems unendingly difficult. But if you do, I pray and hope that when the time comes to accept it, to start getting used to it, you will allow yourself to. We don't want to have to be at that point, of course. But perhaps there, in that dirt of acceptance, is where you can start to plant little strong roots and bloom into something new.

PART 2

Give yourself a lot of grace when going through a pandemic.

DID YOU WATCH SEASON TWO OF *The Morning Show*
on Apple TV? They featured Covid, and it felt too
soon. Enough time simply had not passed to turn it
into entertainment. Because when I tried to watch the
show, I was still smack-dab in the middle of worrying
about if I was going to get the Delta strain (we did), or
the Spirit Airlines strain, or whatever strain the news
was shoving down my throat—or nose? I guess both.
So why would I want to watch a show where Jennifer
Aniston is pretending to do a live newscast with
Covid oozing out of her every perfect pore?[1]

So may I humbly ask if it is still now "too soon" to
discuss Covid? Because I want to, just a wee bit.[2] Even
a decade after the pandemic, it may still feel too soon.
Covid took things from everyone that can never be

---

[1] I still watched the entire season though. It is so good, even with
all the Covid-y pandemic plotlines. Steve Carell in a dramatic
role is always so good. Michael Scott, who? And move over, "I
love lamp," we have serious-business acting to accomplish.
[2] Apparently, I now write with an Irish accent.

given back—milestones, jobs, an optimistic outlook on the future of humanity. Lives, for goodness' sake. But at some point, I guess, we can gently acknowledge that we all, as in the entire WORLD, just walked through something really hard. THE ENTIRE WORLD. AT ONE TIME. That is so wild. And at some point, the entire world will have to move forward from living in Covid, to reflecting and learning from it, right? Maybe?

I know people were hit by Covid a lot harder than our family was. People lost loved ones, and I don't take that lightly at all, by any means. People also grieved the loss of dreams, finances, graduations, weddings, the ability to taste, the ability to watch the news without wanting to run and hide in a cave in Alaska for the rest of your life. It was a lot.

We all have stories, reflections, lessons learned from the pandemic. It will be a time in history that we retell to our grandchildren as we sit in a rocking chair and stare ominously into a campfire. Or as we take a family vacation to the moon and need to pass the time until we land—who knows what the future looks like.

So, here is a little glimpse into my corner of the pandemic pandemonium, and what I learned. Because, like when facing an illness, a death, a bout of loneliness, or a broken relationship—basically anything long and difficult—you have to figure out a way to find joy and stand firm, no matter what is swirling around you.

Hey you. Yeah, you. I hope you can give yourself a bit of credit for all you went through during Covid. It was a lot, for a million different reasons, big and small. And our hearts probably need a bit of healing still. And definitely will forever be changed.

CHAPTER FOUR

Carve out time for your dreams, even in a global crisis.

Have you ever worked toward a dream for a really long time, and then it actually comes true—but it isn't exactly as you imagined it? And do you ever feel guilty for being stressed out over the dream that you fought so long and hard to achieve? I do.

Since I was about twenty years old, I knew I wanted to write books. I self-published one in 2012, but from working in the publishing industry as a publicist, I knew I wanted to publish more traditionally, with an agent and a publisher and the whole shebang. Which is a super difficult, far-fetching dream to have. I knew that, but it didn't stop me.

So, guess what I did? I worked my booty off. Not actually of course—exercise is difficult and my booty is dense. But I worked, and worked, and worked . . . for years. And then more years! I didn't ever really know what the outcome would be, but I *knew* that I had to at least try. I felt so called to writing, and it was the thing that lit my soul up the most. At one point, I even asked God to make me stop wanting to write if it wasn't what was meant for me. I enjoyed it too much! Doesn't the world tell us that serving God looks more like ladling at soup kitchens or moving overseas to work in an orphanage?[1] Writing felt indulgent and sometimes silly.

But what if—possibly—we are all created so uniquely and differently for a purpose? If your dream and calling aren't exactly cookie-cutter then, well, the math lines up. We all have our own weird little thing we love and are good at, so let's lean in to whatever that might be.

After literally praying for God to take away my desire to be an author, I still felt the desire and the calling. Sigh. So, I trusted it, and worked my way forward as best I could. And what that looked like was taking tiny, seemingly insignificant yet very important steps toward what I knew in my heart I felt I was meant to do, without having any idea of what the end game would look like. Jumping into a big black pit of the unknown—that is always fun, right? Nope.

I think it is so important for creatives and creators to remind each other as often as possible that achieving a goal or dream doesn't typically happen in one big, glamorous swoop. Sometimes we think it does because all we see is the shine of success or the viral video that got someone on national TV and changed their life forever. But behind that big, sparkly public moment, they likely had a bunch of grit and grime and work and tears and failures.

The older I get the more I realize that art often happens in the negative spaces surrounding real life. In the fifteen minutes stolen where you work on your lunch break between bites of a subpar turkey sandwich. Or, the early Saturday mornings when your kids are content watching cartoons for a half hour and you take a minute to create and work.

---

[1] It can of course look like that. But sometimes it doesn't.

Art is created in the cracks. It is formed in bits and pieces of stolen time. It's not formed in romantic, peaceful, toddler-free weekends at a quaint B & B by yourself with nothing else to do but write, or paint, or whatever it is that lights you up.

When you realize that and find those cracks, you then realize that you are the only one who can make you do your thing *in* those cracks. I know—annoying, right? The ball is usually in our court. We have to put down our phones, stand up, and take the steps toward our goals. Ugh.

Yes, sometimes a client meeting or report deadline takes precedent. Or perhaps a renegade UFO sighting in your town proves to be quite distracting for a few days. Or sometimes, something takes up all your emotional energy—not just your time. Like a sick child or a terrible new tragedy making headlines that has put you in a deep funk. It's okay to take a pause and care for yourself during those times. And to seek shelter from the aliens for a few days.

Heck, for me sometimes simply taking the time to take a shower seems to use up most of the time I have in the day not dedicated to my kids, husband, and day job.

But I do believe if you can be consistent and persistent, you will get where you want to be. And of course pray over everything along the way, but that's a given.

Something else that helped me as I was working toward my goals and dreams was an accountability buddy. I had a friend, Lauren, who also had a desire to write books. But she, like me, was working and parenting small children, and it all just seemed impossible. She homeschooled and just gave birth to her third child. I worked full-time and just gave birth to my second. There was no way to take time out and meet downtown at a cute coffee shop to spend hours writing to-gether in solidarity.

So we did what we could with what we had. We picked one hour a week that would probably be a wash anyway—Wednesdays at noon. Like honestly, what else are you doing on a Wednesday at noon? We decided to text each other at the beginning of the hour to check in, write at our separate homes miles away from each other, and then check in at the end.

Was it glamorous? Nope. But were we taking the largest steps possible toward reaching our goals and dreams? Yes. We were both moving in the right direction, at the fastest pace we could in that time of our life—which wasn't very fast at all. But it felt great.

I will never forget the first Wednesday at noon when we did this. Leading up to it, I thought of nine hundred different excuses of why I couldn't take an hour of time to work on my writing that day. That one email I should respond to. The dishes! How dare I write if there are *dirty dishes*?[2] I should probably prep dinner for tonight . . . and maybe the next three weeks also just to be efficient. And I am pretty sure that now is the time I need to make that dentist appointment I have been putting off for two years. How can you try and publish a book if you can't even remember to call the dentist?

Any excuse my brain could muster up to try and pull me away from taking one small little stolen hour of time for myself and my art was raging through my brain. These kinds of thoughts are normal. I know that now. I know that they will probably always come. But you have the option to politely (or rudely) tell

-----

[2]Who am I kidding? My sink is always full of dirty dishes and empty cans of store-brand seltzer water.

them to piss off, then do the thing you know you are supposed to do anyway.

Noon came, and *bzz*, a text came in from my friend. I texted her back and forced myself to do the one thing I actually loved doing the most, which is ridiculous but being a human is weird sometimes.

I decided that day to dust off my query letter for my book proposal and take a leap of faith by emailing it out to literary agents . . . again. I had done it before, for what seemed like a million times, with no luck. But I knew that if I wanted to get a book published, the agent was the first step.

When I am not writing books, I am doing PR and consulting for authors on their own publishing journey. I always tell my clients that you need to expect to pitch at least one hundred agents before you might get a positive response. Don't give up or change direction or feel completely defeated until you at least hit one hundred. And I knew I was nowhere near the one-hundred mark yet—so I had to keep trying. I can't cheer on my clients and tell them to keep going, but then not do it myself, right? So, I hit send, yet again, to another agent on my list. Sigh.

But this time, about five minutes later, I received a reply back. The agent, Rachel, was interested in seeing the full proposal. Dude, this almost never happens. Most times you get an answer back a couple of weeks later, if at all, and the answer is usually a "no thanks." Even more common, you hear nothing but silence and the sound of your own despair ringing in your ears. But this time I got a response, and it was positive.

I sent the full proposal, and a few days later Rachel and I jumped on a phone call, and we clicked instantly—another mini miracle—and she signed me on. I told her this story later—how it was the very first day I committed to writing with my friend, in the very first email sent, that we connected. She told me there was no reason for her to be in her email at that time, but she randomly was, and in came my message, fresh and hot at the top of her massive inbox. It all was so oddly perfectly timed that it is so obvious the Lord had a hand on it. Because sometimes he does crazy stuff like that, and I love it.

The reason I am sharing this is because I want to give you a bit of hope when you are chasing after your own big, wild dream. Sometimes the long, hard thing we need to face head-on isn't just a sick child, a financial challenge, or an Alexa that you are pretty sure is spying on you and planning to murder you in your sleep. Sometimes it is just the act of being brave and standing up and fighting for the life that you want. For the dreams that you want to achieve, for the desires of your heart. Sometimes it is just the act of taking small steps in faith and kicking all excuses to the curb as you do so.

What happened that day, at noon on a boring Wednesday, was I simply did everything I could at the time to step a tiny bit closer to what I felt called by God to do. And then he showed up, and took me farther than I could have ever planned on my own. God is able to do more than we can imagine. He is stronger than we realize, in all areas of our life.

But even when things don't happen so seemingly miraculously and instantaneously, the small steps of faith are worth it. Because it is always a no, until the day that it is a yes. Sometimes, continuing to walk in faith is the only thing we have control over.

After a few months of Rachel and me going over my proposal and refining it, it was time for her to start pitching it around to publishers. What resulted was a long, lovely string of "no thank yous." I even had a really promising Zoom meeting with one publisher. We laughed! We bonded! It went great! I really liked her leather bomber jacket! And . . . she still said no.

I read once that J. K. Rowling had Harry Potter rejected by twelve publishers before one said yes. Clearly, I am at the J. K. Rowling–level of writing skills, so I held on to that number.[3] As long as I didn't surpass twelve rejections, there was still hope.

We inched closer and closer. With each rejection, I took about a day to grieve, then kept my chin up as high as I could.[4] But then finally, one day, one publisher said yes. One is all it takes, right? A million noes don't matter, but one yes does.

So with that, I became a traditionally published author.

And guess when I signed my contract?

GUESS. I WANT YOU TO GUESS. BECAUSE IT IS SO FUNNY.

I signed the contract in March of 2020, a.k.a. the month of doom.

About one week exactly after I signed the contract, the entire world shut down. As the pandemic progressed, 90 percent of my mental energy was now wondering things like, *Will I catch this mysterious disease? Will my children? How am I going to work with kids at home? Will my job be affected by all this? Do I have enough toilet paper to get through the week? And why is organic cleaner the only thing available in stores—I NEED CHEMICALS AT A TIME LIKE THIS.*

In my previous daydreams about being a published author, I envisioned my book writing way of life to look something like:

....

[3]This is a joke! Don't come at me, Hufflepuffs.
[4]I actually have two chins so . . . I kept my *chins* held high. I have a weak jawline and always have so whatever. I will embrace it.

Wake up. Drink coffee. Smile. Send the kids to school with a friendly wave. Go to yoga to get all my brain juices at full functioning capacity. Sit down and blissfully write for a few hours. Then, switch to my day job and emails, and welcome the kids home from school with a healthy meal and a calm hug.

Ha. Hahahahahahahahahaha.

Instead, the universe (God?) decided to grant me something my heart has wished and longed for all this time during one of the most tumultuous months in history.

That can't be a coincidence, right? Like of all the months, in all the years, for this to come together—March of 2020?!

My writing life now looked like waking up feeling subpar from stress-drinking red wine the night before. Guzzling as much iced coffee as my nervous system would allow before exploding with anxiety. Parenting two kids who were now home all day, 'errrrrrr day, in addition to working a full-time day job that *luckily* didn't slow down one bit. On weekends we were still really quarantining at this time, so it was just us four—Kyle, Sunny, Shepherd, and me—in the backyard, week after week. It was all very unglamorous, scary, and stressful. I know you know.

Basically—this all felt like the worst time possible to write a book. Or do anything that didn't involve Lysol and watching *Tiger King*.

I am so well aware of how blessed and privileged I was to be home and still work, have my babies and husband home safe with me, and that we were okay and healthy. We never even *fully* ran out of toilet paper—though it got dicey a few days. All of this is not lost on me—I know that it was a lot, lot harder for so many people. People lost their loved ones, their jobs, their relationships. It was all beyond awful.

Adjusting to the pandemic came at varying degrees for everyone, and mine just included having to manage a life that was completely flipped upside down and then writing a book at the exact same time.

But like many difficult things in life, there was no option to avoid it, make it better, or skip over the hard parts. I had to walk right through it—the pandemic and somehow also cranking out coherent thoughts onto paper.

So, how do you create art in a moment like that? At a time where twenty-six out of the twenty-four hours a day were dedicated to taking care of kids, joining Zoom calls, and hunting down disinfectant products in the wild while not catching a deadly virus, armed with nothing but a homemade facemask, an almost-empty hand-sanitizer bottle, and fear.

I think that dream chasing and achieving always ends up being a bit less glamorous than we expect. It isn't ever long, perfect writing sessions after lovely yoga classes. Rather, it is little bits of work here and there, whenever you can fit it in. It is taking fifteen minutes in the morning to pray, quieting every excuse telling you not to do the thing you are called to do, and then just forcing yourself to do it.

That is what writing a book in 2020 taught me. Art most often is simply created in cracks of life. It is formed in bits and pieces of stolen time. Most times that is all we get, so take it and use it.

Writing a book in 2020 also taught me something else. One would think that adding such a huge task to an already full workweek and life schedule would add more stress, but it in fact did the opposite. Writing became the best part of my day. The one thing at that time that made me feel like *me* again, when everything else around me was so unsure.

Writing, even if only for a bit, gave me energy to get through the rest of the day, Zoom meeting by Zoom meeting, snack request by snack request. It made me happy and feel like myself again. And maybe that is enough?

So often we make every excuse to skip over the things that actually light our souls up and fuel them to better tackle the hard stuff, which seems silly. So no matter what life is throwing at you, I hope you can fight to make the time for the good stuff in life, even if in the cracks. Because I do believe that your happiness, your joy, your soul lighting up to fully enjoy this life is worth it. Even if things don't roll out exactly as you had planned, your spirit might be a little bit brighter, which is, well, important.

At the time of writing this, the pandemic is mostly okay? I think? Hard to say. People still get "The Vid," but it is better than it was. Our faces are unmasked, the kids are happy at school, and the most recent variant gracing the headlines— which we of course caught—wasn't *that* awful. It was mostly just obnoxious, and I will take that over deadly any day. But even now, with more time and mental space, I still have to force myself to make time to write, to create, to do anything for myself. And I think it will probably always be like that, right? We can make excuses, we can stay distracted, but when it comes down to it, we have to make a choice to take the time, even if it is just in the tiniest bits and pieces. But it's worth it.

So I hope we can all get more comfortable with that. Get comfortable with the fact that, yes, twenty minutes in a car pickup line of writing, or business-plan building, or needle-pointing borderline inappropriate statements onto cloth napkins, or just taking a breath isn't necessarily glamorous. But it is there, that little pocket of time for the taking, so I hope we can all snatch it up in the best way possible.

When God calls you to something—a dream, an art, a passion—maybe he doesn't exactly part the Red Sea so you can casually stroll your way there toward your desired destination. I wish he did! But we all know that isn't true, unless your name is Moses and you have a staff that miraculously turns into a snake, which is a very rare combo these days. Maybe sometimes, for whatever reason, God expects you to try to navigate your way with a little bit of faith keeping you afloat.

May we all build a boat on that faith, ride whatever waves come at us (freaking world pandemics included, apparently), and keep paddling toward a life that we love. A life where we don't hold anything back. Where we show up every day, as gently and best we can, trying to be and give the best version of ourselves—whatever that may look like. If it feels indulgent, then do it for others. Do it for the people who will benefit from your words, your gifts, the unique perspective you bring to the world. And do it for the glory of God. Because that isn't indulgent or silly—that is everything.

As Covid and a million other difficult things over the past couple of years have shown us, life is so precious, fragile, and short. So we should make the best out of whatever days, breaths, and moments of time we have. Because they are all such a gift. You are a gift. And the world is ready for whatever beauty you have to add to it.

·····································

CHAPTER FIVE

If you are missing your spouse, simply hide behind a houseplant.

Sometimes, even though our hearts and minds wish that things were bigger, brighter, farther ahead, or freer, we are stuck where we are at, at least for the time being. Lame! But it happens. Have you ever felt that way? Flat-out stuck, with no real physically possible way to adapt your circumstances, so you had to just adapt your attitude, expectations, and what you could control? Sigh. So annoying.

I think that the pandemic, especially very early on, really made people experience that. One week we had the ability to go out, see the world, be with our loved ones and carry on normally with our lives. Then the next, we simply didn't. Everything was different and restricted. Plans were broken and things were to be grieved, small and large.

For our family in March of 2020, we were living in our little home on the end of a crowded neighborhood street in West Palm Beach. It was a two-story home and wood-framed, which are both things they tell you not to have in Florida—the two stories because of hurricanes, and the wood frame because of termites, and, well, hurricanes—but it was all we could afford. It had lasted decades before our family inhabited it, and it was painted the lightest shade of pink—subtly flamingo you might say. And it was nestled under large avocado trees that produced so much fruit my neighbors would sneak over and steal right off them.[1] We loved our home, and we could pay the mortgage on it, so there ya go. It was our little tiny slice of paradise, until well, it was the *only* slice of paradise we were allowed to experience.

No longer were we able to go downtown, to our offices or coffee shops or schools. Church even felt scary! And large social gatherings—don't even think about it, unless you wanted to be publicly shamed. It was just us, our little pink home with way too many avocados, Netflix, and the occasional Uber Eats delivery to support our local diner down the street.

While so many things were challenged, tried, and tested in that time, relationships were certainly one of them. Being stripped of all distractions and vices and left to be with your one person, day in and day out, was complicated. I think any situation where human beings, no matter how much they love each other, are put under mass amounts of stress and forced to live and breathe the same air that may or may not have a mystery virus floating in it is going to be a rough go.

Kyle and I used to live—and work—out of a four-hundred-square-foot apartment in New York City. Ha. Hahahaha. If only 2014 Katie and Kyle knew what 2020 was to bring. Because even though our apartment was so small that we had to hang pots on the wall for storage, we had the ability to, well,

....

[1]Please know they were not Hass avocados but Florida avocados, which unfortunately are just not the same, and I was always sad about it. They are not great for guac, or much of anything except the novelty of having avocados in your yard. I did have one neighbor ask if she could have some to make a hair mask, which seemed like a great yet gross idea.

exit it. And, we also didn't have two toddlers running around screaming and covered in mysterious stickiness and cracker crumbs. Now, in our almost-flamingo-pink home, with about a thousand square feet of more space, it felt even tighter than our micro-apartment did.

The early pandemic was a very physical example of being stuck in a place and a period of time that you would never choose on your own accord. We would never voluntarily say, "Hey, for the next six months let's stay home around the clock, forgo going to the beach, to see our friends, to church, to anywhere we love really, and only enter into a store wearing a HAZMAT suit if we are feeling like risking our life that day." I mean, I suppose perhaps this sounds like a dream to some introverts. But only if they *choose* this way of life. It loses appeal if you are forced to experience it.

Nobody asked for all that mess, but we all had to walk through it anyway. Yet another lesson in having to somehow figure out how to not just survive but also enjoy life a bit, when there was no clear end in sight to the hardships.

Kyle and I were both able to work from home and keep our kids there with us safe—something we knew we were so blessed to be able to do. Eventually, we got into our daily groove and routine: wake up, drink coffee, take a shower if it had been an alarming number of days since our last, quickly discuss who had a meeting when and how we would swap parenting out for all that, then dive right into the grind. After work it was mostly more of the same. Parenting our two babes in the same little house, but with less email to distract us, up until bedtime. All in all, this was tolerable for a couple weeks—because it was all going to blow over soon . . . right? WRONG.

At some point just cruising through life on the back of toler-ability becomes, well, intolerable. Because life is meant to be more than just a bland pattern of humdrum routines, boredom, Zoom calls, and toddler bedtime struggles—rinse and repeat. I do believe in my heart that there is so much beauty and juiciness and sparkle in life that is available for us to tap into, if we look for it. Dare I say in any circumstance? Too optimistic? Let's settle on *in most circumstances.*

But how do you do that when you are confined to a cramped home packed with tiny dictators and a demanding day job of staring at people with weird greenscreen backgrounds?

In life, there is always beauty able to be grasped. But some-times we just need to work a bit harder to find it, savor it, and hang on tight to the memory when it is gone. Sometimes we might even need to whip out a joy-finding metal detector and happiness excavator kit just to find it. But hey—it is better than just staying buried in the crustiness of the mundane.

It can seem easy for life to become a hamster wheel of the same ol' same ol', right? In a global pandemic, or a busy-yet-boring season of nose-to-the-grindstone parenting. Even now, with mask mandates lifted, my kids happily back at school, and things back to a regular routine, if I don't fight back against it, I can feel my body getting heavy under the weight of responsi-bility, parenting, working, adulting, you know ... all the *-ing* things that can become a lot.

What about feeling truly alive, even during times that seem plain? What about feeling connected to and in love with your spouse, even when confined to a small home of chaos? What about feeling inspired and energized and fully present and ex-cited about simply living? Do those things leave once you cross over the age of thirty and your plate is full of responsibilities that sometimes resemble cold mushy vegetables?

No. The good stuff is still obtainable. It just takes a bit of effort to get into the path of inspiration and fuzzy soul feelings.

After a month or two . . . then three or four . . . of pandemic lockdown, Kyle and I were feeling all the blahs. It isn't easy maintaining a marriage while raising two small kids under typical circumstances, let alone during a seemingly unending season of working-parenting-worrying-quarantining. But we sure tried. So, a few months in when we were really feeling weary of the circumstances, Kyle and I did something so simple to work a little bit of joy into our lives, in the smallest way but basically the only way that was available to us at the time.

We hid behind a houseplant.

Okay, listen. In our kinda-pink house, we had gotten into the groove of our weird new apocalyptic way of living, I suppose. We were "doing okay" physically and on paper, but our souls felt like they were puttering along like a *Walking Dead* zombie. Yes, we were managing our work schedules and parenting two very active kids without the ability to take them to a playground, but we felt dull. Lackluster. A bit sad. And very bored. And I *really* hate being bored.

So, we decided to shift our focus. We began to stop focusing on what we no longer had and instead focused on what we still did have. The concept is similar to the end of a grocery week when you are trying to piece together a meal with very random foods. *Yes, I no longer have my kids' favorite chicken nuggets, but I do have old, slightly stale bread, eggs, and cinnamon, so French toast for dinner it is!*

What *did* we have access to in that moment that could light us up a little bit? How could we create a small pocket of joy and delight, in the midst of a global crisis confining us to our cramped home? It was easier then, and honestly even now, to focus on what we don't have We were not able to go out on a date downtown like we used to. We couldn't host a little dinner with our favorite friends and let the kids run free while we relaxed and laughed and talked with other adults. We couldn't do much of anything that didn't involve our backyard or living room. So, we decided to just create the ambiance of what we would be experiencing out in the world, but do it *in*.

One night a week Kyle and I would feed the kids dinner early and hold off on eating ourselves, except for the tiny bites of macaroni we would steal off their plates, obviously. We would put them to bed as early as possible, and then afterward we would head to the kitchen where we would cook a fun meal together—something new, not our usual. For just one day, we would forgo a leftover chicken situation and cook something a bit fancier. Something that we probably would have ordered out if we'd had that option. Kyle and I would sear steaks and sprinkle blue cheese on them, make bacon green beans, pour tall glasses of champagne, put on Bessie Smith radio, light a candle, and then get the magical houseplant.

How the plant worked was we would set it right in the middle of our kitchen table so it blocked out the view of the rest of our house. All we could see were each other, the candle, and our meal, for the most part. It helped us to mentally and physically have a barrier between us and the rest of our messy home—our messy lives. Kyle and I would pretend that next to us wasn't a discarded pile of stuffed animals, but a fancy couple we were

pretending not to eavesdrop on but were 100 percent eaves-
dropping on. We would ignore the pile of laundry in the living
room corner that our dog had now turned into his bed, and
instead comment on how lovely our snake plant was and how
good our meal was. We forced ourselves to take a minute to
enjoy each other, and enjoy life itself, in whatever capacity we
had at that moment. And, yes, I mean forced. Because you know
what would have been easier? More stupid *Tiger King* watching
and stress wine sipping, obviously.

Kyle and I never regretted pushing ourselves a bit to create
the time and space for each other. We never regretted taking
that time to sit, breathe, and connect. To remember why we got
married in the first place—because we actually liked each other,
not because we were half-decent at trying to survive a pandemic
together. And we remembered that we had a life and relationship
before Pull-Ups, wet wipes, and endless episodes of *Paw Patrol*.[2]
That we, as real breathing human beings, were a couple, and we
were individuals before we were parents. In those little stolen
moments, Kyle and I were drawn together, simply relishing the
goodness and love and joy that we still had access to, even if it
took a bit more effort to unearth it.

I like to think back on that silly houseplant, that steak ordered
from Aldi that we wiped with Clorox wipes, and that cheap
bottle of champagne that was perfectly cold.[3] It was a time when
Kyle and I, in our desperation and boredom, did all we could to
make life a bit more beautiful. We couldn't do much, but we

---

[2]The Mighty Pups season is the best.
[3]Please know I mean wiped the steak package with Clorox wipes, not the
 steak itself. I was desperate to avoid a virus, but not at the level of potential poisoning.

could do something. And I want to do that again—today, now, tomorrow. Always.

Some seasons of life, all you can really achieve is "good enough." But maybe good enough sometimes is, well, good enough. I will forever keep reminding myself to fight for little slivers of joy. I will forever remind myself to take advantage of the little good moments, until the big good moments come back around. Because they do. Just on their own schedule sometimes.

So today, if you are feeling the blahs—in your marriage, in your everyday schedule and routine and responsibilities—I hope you will find a houseplant to hide behind, block out whatever mess it is you are dealing with, and focus on the beauty and love right in front of you, if only for a bit. Maybe in this season, that is the best you can do. But that is okay. It is better than doing nothing at all, right?

Life is fleeting and sweet, even during pandemics that seem to go on forever, or long, hard parenting seasons, or facing an illness, or whatever. It kinda all feels slow and fast at the same time. But we can fight for some beauty, we really can. Because the alternative is pretty dang lame. So put up the plant, eat the steak, and enjoy.

CHAPTER SIX

....

Find your yellow Windex.

One of the fun parts of the early pandemic was how going to the grocery store was always an exciting adventure.[1] Will we have to stand in a line to be let into the store like we were waiting for rations during the Depression? Should we wear gloves? Is that still a thing or is it weird now? Will this mask my grandmother knit out of antique, dusty yarn she found in her basement do the trick to block out this raging, deadly virus? Is the person over there wearing a full-on bubble suit actually the smartest of us all, or just very strange? Will there be toilet paper on the shelves or will we have to steal it from the public restrooms in desperation? It was all a mixed bag of chaos, really. There were a lot of questions to be had, with very little answers. We were collectively trying to do our best in this very odd, very apocalyptic-feeling new world with no rule book.

Now listen up—I am not good at cleaning. I did not inherit that gene from my mom, who is great at it. She tried to pass it along, to teach me the ways, but it didn't stick. My room always was—and still is—a complete train wreck. But I saw a TikTok that said if your messy space doesn't bother you or anyone you

....

[1] I say "fun" in the most sarcastic way possible. Just want to make that very, very clear.

live with, then that is fine, keep it messy. And honestly, my messy room doesn't bother me, so I stopped beating myself up about it. I keep the rest of my house as clean as possible for my kids and husband, but my room often looks like it was ransacked by rabid raccoons.

But apparently, when there was a pandemic flying around the world, I suddenly had the urge to scrub the bacterial life out of everything and anything in sight. I finally understood why some people stress-clean their homes. I mean, there is something to that, really. Working through all your anxieties and killing any and every germ possible instead of just putting all your anxieties into a massive bowl of microwave popcorn and a crime show marathon. Cleaning, at least, is a bit more productive.

Even though I had the newfound urge to wipe down my entire home until it shined brighter than Mr. Clean's bald head, there was a slight problem—Mr. Clean appeared to have gone into the witness protection program. He was flat-out gone from the stores. In fact, there were no products in the store that killed any sort of germ. Was there organic stuff that made your counter smell good with essential oils? Sure! But there was nothing that sanitized, and in a pandemic, you kinda really want that germ-fighting, complete-opposite-of-organic, all-the-chemical-and-fumes killing power that the good old chemists of America have conjured up in the last two decades. But alas, only froufrou, healthy-for-you-and-the-environment, lovely smelling sprays were to be had. Darn. But I guess bring on the lavender essential oils if you must.

Oh, what I would have given to see that cartoon's shining bald head on a bottle. I might have kissed his little fake face right there in the store, if it weren't for well, ya know, masks and

Covid. What a cool way to ramp up your anxieties over germs: take away anything that can *kill* germs and leave us confused and practically defenseless. Thanks, world, you cruel beast.

So, here we were again in another tough situation where we had no option but to adapt, adjust, figure it out. Sensing a theme here? Whether it be a lack of cleaning supplies or a lack of health or a lack of security or relationships or whatever— sometimes you just have to take a detour from what you had expected and planned for. You have to really plainly ask God for help, guidance, and provision, even when you don't really know how it's possible.

And yes, this is a chapter about cleaning supplies and the Lord, all mixed together. Just roll with it, okay? Things got really weird in 2020. I know you know. Nothing was off the table—the unsanitized table, that is.

So one day, when I was at Walmart, masked up and essentially looking like I was about to perform a semi-sterile surgery while also feeling like at any moment a zombie might emerge from the produce section, God did provide. Provision for my germ situation descended from above with a golden glow, piercing through the sad darkness of the near-empty metal store shelves. Was this ball of shimmering yellow majesty a literal angel of the Lord, towering over us to give us a divine word? Nope! But close. It was a bottle of yellow Windex on the top shelf of the grocery store. And it was a disinfectant. *Cue the "Hallelujah Chorus."*

When you think of Windex, you likely just associate a chemically aggressive–smelling glass cleaner that makes squeaky sounds when being wiped and doesn't work that well. Windex, along with all the other non-germ-killing cleaners, never went out of stock during the pandemic. Sure, your kitchen counter may have been bursting with bacteria and viruses, but at least your glass items would sparkle. But for some reason that day at Walmart, as I gazed at the blue bottles of Windex in annoyance, I saw a yellow bottle sitting right next to it. Same brand—straight-up Windex through and through, but it was yellow and it said "all-purpose cleaner." *Odd*, I thought. I thought Windex was more in the market of helping nosy neighbors get a clear view of the latest tea, not countertop cleaning. So I grabbed the yellow bottle and read further and—gasp—it said in small letters it killed 99.9 percent of germs. This was the most attractive statement one could say in the midst of a global virus catastrophe.

Was I dreaming? Was I being Punk'd by an aging Ashton Kutcher? Did Covid cause hallucinations? Nope. None of those options. Windex apparently did make a disinfectant cleaner, but just had a subpar marketing team and label, because nobody knew about it. I sure didn't! Never knew about it, never heard of it. And evidenced by the multiple bottles left on the store shelf, others didn't either. While people just assumed the yellow liquid was going to make their windows smell like a lemon and passed right over it, it actually could kill germs—the one thing we all needed so badly at that time. Listen, this yellow Windex wasn't shouting from the rooftops: I AM THE BEST GERM BLASTER IN ALL THE LANDS like Mr. Clean's shiny head does. It was just sitting there, as it always had been, overlooked but quietly reliable.

I grabbed a bottle and debated giving it a hug before I dropped it in my cart, but I resisted. I did try to awkwardly tell the other sad-looking patrons in the cleaning aisle, "Hey—this stuff disinfects!" But it got weird because it's hard to communicate through masks, and nobody wants to be spoken to in the dank isles of Walmart anyway, especially during a pandemic. But at least I tried.

So, I went home with my new yellow friend and sprayed basically everything possible in our home. It felt great to disinfect, like I at least had a tiny bit of control over what was happening inside my four walls. This bottle of yellow Windex was a small, golden-hued blessing in the midst of a lot of gray, germy days.

When we went to a different grocery store later that week, I decided to check if the yellow Windex was just a one-time fluke—perhaps the Windex delivery truck arrived just before my fated Walmart trip. But nope! Even at a new store, next to the bottles of blue, sitting again on mostly empty shelves were several bottles of the yellow. Golden nuggets of cleaning prowess.

People didn't know that what they were searching for was there right in front of them all along.

Again and again, anytime we went to a store for the next few months I would check for the yellow Windex, and it was always there—a consistent beacon of light and hope. Even as things eased up a bit and felt a little more normal, and Mr. Clean's shiny head was yet again present among the shelves, I still reached for the yellow Windex.

Because look.

The yellow Windex was consistent. It never left, even when times got really hard. It wasn't the loudest or flashiest bean in the bunch, by any means. But it was reliable, there when you needed it, and got the job done.

You guys. We all need a yellow Windex in our lives. But in human form. And, we can even strive to be the yellow Windex for others. The person who is reliable, consistent. Someone who is always there to help the people they love. Someone who is ready to roll their sleeves up when things get messy, no bald head required.

Yellow Windex was there for me when nothing else was. Was she trendy and organic? Nope. But she showed up time and again. I think in hard times of life, sometimes the flashy, the fun, the fancy peel away. What we are left with is what and who really matters. The people who will be there for you when the bottom of your life falls out and you are just a mess on the floor needing a little help getting back up again.

With the pandemic taking away so much excess from us and really boiling down our lives and relationships, it illuminated what and who was really important to us. I feel forever changed by it. It showed me the ability to adapt when we had less. The ability to appreciate just what was right in front of you, what and who was consistent in your life. The ones you were hunkering down with as you were fighting back against whatever the world was going to throw at you during such an unknown time.

I hope now, as we have stumbled back into a rhythm of normalcy, we can still pause to recognize who in our lives will be there, no matter what. Who are the people who are quietly reliable, trustworthy, and comfortable—and possibly also smell lemony fresh because that can't hurt? And who are we that person *for*? How can we better become the friend, the spouse, the daughter, or the parent who remains a consistent soft place to land for the ones holding a big stake of real estate in our heart? How can we be the yellow Windex for others, shining down a little gleam of golden light when everything else seems gray and empty?

Appreciate your yellow Windex people. Be the yellow Windex person for others. Hug the yellow Windex in life. Just don't drink the yellow Windex, and everything will be okay.

PART 3

Raising small human creatures is a wild journey.

PARENTING SMALL HUMAN BEINGS IS like having a heart made out of glittery slime and it being stretched in opposite directions, as far as possible, all at once. Never has anything made me feel as much joy and love as my children have. And nothing has ever made me feel more defeated, exhausted, and frustrated. How can that wide range of emotions come from the same source? The disparity between loving something so deeply but also having that love be one of the most challenging things in your life is just flat-out wild. It makes little sense, yet also makes complete sense. Does that . . . make sense?

It isn't just having kids that teaches you things through trial, of course. There are other things in life that are hard yet refine you as you walk through them. Before having kids, I was refined through things like grief, financial struggle, navigating marriage, having to fully trust the Lord with a new city, a new chapter, a fresh start. Now, the refinement is mostly just working on not losing my cool in the midst of an absurd amount of overstimulating, loud sounds and constant snack requests. And, of course, all the other big scary medical stuff with Shepherd, but that is a bonus stressor. A little stress icing on the stress cake, if you will.

I think parenting is a really simple yet deeply complex way for God to teach us deep life lessons. To stretch us further than we ever thought our slimy, sparkly hearts could go. But when they do stretch, wow. It is pretty beautiful.

....

CHAPTER SEVEN

Remember that God loves our kids too.

One minute you are in the hospital holding your first baby, and then you sneeze and find yourself parenting a kindergartner who has the audacity to ride a bus to school all by themself. How dare they be so grown and independent! Get back in the swaddle and let's snuggle, please! From the dawn of time until the end of the world, I think all parents will ask this question—how does this go by so fast?

That is exactly what I was thinking as I was sitting on the front porch of my home on the morning of my daughter Sunny's fifth birthday. I was reading the Bible and praying for her and about her. I was thanking God over and over for her sweet, precious life, and all the joy she brought to our family. Also, I was praying he would surround her with angels, keep her safe, and protect her fiercely. Because five just felt like such a different chapter of childhood. She was basically a big kid now—the toddler days were in the past, the preschool days in the past. I knew this year was going to be a big season of growing and independence for her. And I was excited! But it also meant more freedom, more doing things on her own while I watched from afar. And that is a scary thing for a parent's heart.

I was thinking and praying and rocking in our little front-porch chair when something slipped out of the pages of my Bible. It was an ultrasound picture of Sunny I had forgotten was even in there. Something I had tucked away years ago right after an appointment, not even realizing it was there despite reading that Bible countless times since. The fact that it was that exact moment I was reflecting on and praying for my sweet little lady's life when it fell out felt very significant.

I was looking at the little picture—mostly just a gray and black blob in the shape of something resembling an alien-human hybrid—when I realized this wasn't just a regular old ultrasound picture. It was an extra special one, and I felt sure that God was speaking to me.

Kyle and I had lost our first baby—the one before Sunny—when we were about ten weeks pregnant. It was absolutely heartbreaking and we grieved deeply. But when the time came to do so, we tried again. When chasing something that was so deeply woven into my soul, I felt all I could do was stand up, face the hard thing, and simply try again. We did get pregnant for a second time and were so grateful.

Soon I realized that because of our previous miscarriage, I was scared this one wasn't going to stick around either. It wasn't even a conscious choice, really, but a subconscious level of anxiety that I could not shake. Rationally, I knew things would probably, statistically, be okay, but the amount of fear I felt took me by surprise.

Everything with this new baby cooking in my belly was going perfectly on paper. The doctor had put me on progesterone supplements because we had tested my hormones right away and apparently my levels were low, which likely contributed to my first loss. The baby was trucking along just fine, with a strong heartbeat, meeting all the growth markers. Things felt stronger, more typical this time. Despite all that, every time I went to the bathroom, I would brace myself for the sight of blood in my underwear. And every doctor's appointment I felt like my own heart stopped beating until the ultrasound showed my tiny child dancing around on the screen

After going through a loss so devastating before, it was like my body was building up an adrenaline defense system, constantly on guard against something it had no control over. My mind and body were trying with all their might to prevent the bad thing from happening again, even though I knew consciously it was totally and utterly out of my control.

Even though it was so scary, I knew if I was going to have another child, I was just going to have to feel those awful feelings and keep walking forward anyway. This is so often the case with many big, important things in life, right? It isn't easy, having to trust the Lord with something so unbelievably precious to your heart. Something that didn't work out before. But there is no other option except to walk through the hard thing with as much hope as you can hold on to along the way.

So, Kyle and I more or less held our breaths collectively for about the first trimester of our pregnancy. We made it past the week we lost our first child and were able to breathe a tiny bit more. Then we made it to the golden twelve-week mark where miscarriage becomes significantly less likely, and we were happy. But also still scared. Dang it, feelings.

At the time, when we hit that significant week, we were living out of state so Kyle could perform as Hamlet for a summer Shakespeare festival. To be or not to be . . . a real cute squishy baby in our future . . . that is the question. We were away from our normal ob-gyn, which was fine because we weren't scheduled for appointments during those weeks anyway. But when that twelve-week mark came, I wanted to tell the world, "Hey! I am a woman with a baby on board!" This one seemed like they would be sticking around for good, but without recent confirmation from a doc that all was well, I couldn't help but worry. What if something was wrong, and I just didn't know because we hadn't had an appointment for a couple weeks? Was the baby *actually* okay in there? I felt I just had to know for sure, before we told anyone the news. My heart and brain needed official confirmation before the celebration.[1] And I really wanted the celebration, especially after such heartache the first time around.

I began to call local doctors and explain our weird situation. I am sure my nervous rambling calls with talks of miscarriages and Hamlet and wanting an ultrasound just this one time sounded really strange. A few practices said they wouldn't see me. *What—you don't regularly scan completely random women whose husbands work the summer Shakespeare festival circuit?* Rude. But I didn't give up. Then one office I called simply said, "Sure, why not? Come on in, you anxious weirdo." I may be a little dramatic on the exact wording there, but they threw me an ultrasound bone, and I was grateful.

So Kyle and I went in, got the ultrasound, and everything was fine. Such joy! As simple as that. The baby was okay, and we felt like we could finally fully exhale, tell everyone we knew, and celebrate the amazing blessing. The office handed us a few

---

[1]Rhyming is fun. Sorry, I'm done. Anybody want a peanut?

printed-out images of our baby that I held close to my heart, shared with everyone I knew, and eventually tucked deep into my Bible for safekeeping as we traveled back to our home at the end of the summer and continued preparing to have our child.

Sometimes in life, things go so smoothly, and have a really positive outcome. Yes, there are sometimes complexities, death, and heartbreak. But just the same, there are times of great happiness and ease. Of blessing and grace and just sheer goodness. And sometimes, the seasons even overlap a bit. Just as easy as things can be scary and bad and hard, they can also go really well, be simple and joyful. It is so important to savor those moments because often they can carry you a long way. There is so much that deserves to be celebrated in life, simply because there is so much that does not. For me, when times are difficult or hard, I like to think back on the times that were just good, and remind myself I was there before and can be there again. And, when I am there again, I will be counting my blessings even more.

Our little baby in my belly, who would grow to be our fierce little Sunny, turned out to be an easy blessing after a time of hardship and loss. Something good after we walked through something really bad. I think when we are gifted those times and moments, we should completely and fully appreciate them. We should mark them in our minds and hearts, make notes to tuck away so we can look back at them and remember the goodness of God. The beauty of life. This time of extreme good shone so brightly it made the times of dark less visible.

So there, five years later on the front porch of our home, listening to the giggles of my now two children and Kyle drifting through the front window, that little anxiety-ridden ultrasound photo reminded me of just how far we had come. And, I clearly felt God in that moment whisper in my heart, reminding me he has loved Sunny since *then*. Since the time she was a little bean in my belly and I was praying so hard for her to thrive, just like I was praying so hard for her now, five years later, and will be for the rest of my life. God has loved her since before I even knew her, and he will love her forever. His hand was on her then, and is on her now.

I needed that reminder. It felt like a nice warm, comforting hug. The warm part could have been the eighty-degree Florida heat on my front porch, but who is to say. I needed the reminder of how God loves my kids—all our kids—*so* much. It isn't just my meager love trying to wrap her up and protect her—it is his also. And that is a powerful thing.

I love when God sends tiny reminders to us about where we have come from and what we have walked through, so we can better appreciate just how amazingly he has shown up for us in the now. That little photo, adorned with the name of the doctor I only ever saw one random time, reminded me of just how scared I was then. But also how God was with me every step of the journey, and still is to this day. He cared about every single one of Sunny's tiny heartbeats inside my belly, and every single one of hers now as she continues forward as the beautiful curly-haired firecracker she is.

And guess what—it isn't just Sunny's heart and life God cares about. That would be weird. He also cares about you. And even me and my mess too. I believe God loved us when we were the tiny alien beings on the fuzzy ultrasound screen just as much as he does now. Before we could even comprehend that love, before we could even say or understand the word *love*.

No matter what we are facing today, we can rest in that love. We can rest in remembering God was with us since before we ever took our first breath, and he will be with us until we take our last, and beyond. His love is big, for us and for our kids. And that is, well, everything.

CHAPTER EIGHT

Chill out about parenting, especially during a modern-day apocalypse.

Sunny was having an epic, all-out, inconsolable meltdown. She wasn't in trouble, and from what I could see nothing really happened to set her off, but she was sobbing. I wanted to make the tears stop, but nothing seemed to help. I figured she was just tired and so I was trying to expedite bedtime so homegirl could get some rest. Despite my efforts, sleep was not to be had, just more and more weeping. It was breaking my heart. Also slightly infuriating me—parenting is such a juxtaposition. But mostly breaking my heart. As a parent, you will do anything to fix whatever problem your babies are having. Except sometimes they can't or won't tell you what that problem is, which is so hard.

Sunny continued crying and wailing, and I continued trying all my tricks to cheer her up to no avail. Telling her I saw a really crazy-colored iguana that day doing something strange usually works—feel free to follow me for more expert-level parenting advice. But she didn't care about my dumb fake iguana story. She didn't want her back rubbed, a snack, to read a book, anything. So, I ended up just begging her to tell me what was wrong as my heart broke a little bit more with each of her cries. I wanted to fix it, but I had no idea where to begin.

My mom brain naturally went to all the worst-case scenarios of what she was crying about, and I was pretty sure I knew. It was just a few months into the pandemic, and there was still so much she was adjusting to. She was no longer at her school she loved, playing with her friends she loved. She wasn't even able to see her cousins, which we usually do every weekend. Even the beach was closed! We were confined to our little house and backyard for any form of entertainment. A backyard that had a lot of mosquitos. She had to wear a mask anytime we went anywhere, which we rarely did, and she had to deal with her parents being on Zoom calls all day at home. It was a lot. It was a lot for a grownup who had a (mostly) reasonable grasp on their emotions, let alone a five-year-old.

So as she continued crying, I was sure—dare I say positive— that all the stress and trauma from having her life instantly flipped upside down was what was bothering her. I mean, she was now just stuck at home with two full-time working parents who were confused and worried about what the heck this virus was, what was going to happen, and just having their worry increase with every viewing of the nightly news, which suddenly had turned into an apocalyptic sci-fi film.

I was scared for her. For her sweet little heart and how all this change and stress would affect her. Five-year-olds should be worried about how many more episodes of *Bluey* they are allowed to watch before bed and exactly when the next time they will get to eat a cupcake is, not if they will catch "the sickness" that apparently is so bad that even the neighborhood playground is off-limits and wrapped in yellow caution tape.

As she cried, and I was unable to console her, I began to cry also because if you can't beat them join them.[1] We were just two crying gals, unsure about what was happening in the universe, and what would be happening next.

But then finally—*gasp*. Sunny calmed down a slight bit. I could see in her eyes that she was just about ready to tell me what was bothering her. She was finally getting ready to share, and oh boy, was I ready to listen. *Bring it on, lady! Tell Mom all the feels you feel. I will do everything I can to make it better. Let's discuss. Let's hash it out.* I was bracing myself for her to say something super dramatic like, "I am scared of the sickness," or "I just want to go back to school and see my friends," or "Why are we all stuck at home all the time?"

I was sure she was going to ask a big hard question that there was no good answer to. Or, she would share a big real fear that she had about the pandemic that I was probably also feeling myself. My mom heart clenched in worry and anticipation as Sunny began to talk between cries. I was at the ready to comfort, explain, console—whatever she needed.

"I am upset because . . ." Here we go. The big sad moment. She continued, "I am mad because you beat me at UNO earlier today."

And with that, she began to wail again with maximum force.

Oh. My. Gosh. Here I was thinking that Sunny was worried about the current awful state of the world, about what was going to happen to us, about why her life was completely

----

[1]This is not real parenting advice, but sometimes a mom's gotta cry. But telling them dramatically about the "iguana" you saw that day oddly does usually work to distract them from big feelings. Don't question my methods, just embrace them.

upended and if it would ever go back to normal. NOPE. She was mad that I won our game of UNO that happened a solid six hours prior.

Let's unpack this.

It can be so hard as a parent to love someone more than your own life, with every fiber of your being and then some, but realize you do not have complete control over their happiness. And no matter how you swing it, their happiness is so closely intertwined with your own. If they are sad, you are likely also sad. If they hurt, you hurt so deeply too. We can do all that we can for these creatures, these sweet babies that we love more than anything, but at the same time so much is out of our hands. So much of our lives and emotions are things that we are not able to tangibly fix or help with. And that is hard.

And I do expect that it gets even harder as time goes on. Because if it hurt my heart to see my young daughter weep over a lost game of UNO, what will it be like when she cries to me about a bully in middle school or her first breakup? How will my mom heart even handle that?

But I am not there yet. I am here, leaning over her little pink twin bed, wiping her tears and assuring her that "Hey, we can play UNO again tomorrow, and you can try again to kick my butt, which most times you do anyway."

Yes, the pandemic was so hard and awful. It really did have an effect on kids—especially older ones who lost out on so many important memories and milestones and were able to fully understand the stress of what was happening. At the same time, it also showed us just how resilient kids are. How strong and adaptable they can be when needed, and that was an amazing thing to see.

I feel like one of the most beautiful surprises about having kids, or even just spending time with them, is that God gives us so many lessons through their sweet little simple hearts. We could all benefit from striving to be like them, more focused on exactly what is in front of us and in this moment—the here and now. Caring more about our games of UNO, not the unending amount of questions we can't control or know the answers to. Perhaps there is profound wisdom and strength in the way their little brains operate—focusing on what is right in front of them. The love that surrounds them. The fun that can be had.

Of course, it is easy to say that, and then add on a hundred adult excuses like, "But I have bills to pay, bro. And I have yard work. And have you seen the state of the economy? We are all doomed." And I get that, sure. But it can only be a good thing for us to take the time to slow down and recognize the wisdom in taking each moment as it comes. To focus on the blessings and goodness and happiness that is right in front of us in this very moment at this very time, instead of having our eyes drift to the wide, open, scary unknown of what might happen tomorrow.

And, especially under the stress of a global crisis, perhaps we can lighten up on ourselves about parenting. How is that for a parenting book title? *Relax, the Kids are Fine . . . Probably.* Seems very 1990s parenting-esque, and since nineties fashion is coming back, maybe this will take off too.

But maybe every single difficult thing our kids face isn't going to destroy their emotional well-being. Maybe it will just build up their character, just like the hard things we face do to us. I hope that we can all give ourselves a little more grace in parenting. I hope we can trust that our unending love for these babies will somehow, someway, simply be enough.

Also, sometimes I do let Sunny beat me in games, but sometimes I just go ham and kick her butt without mercy. Depends on the day. But if we play checkers, she destroys me every time. And don't get me started on her secret tic-tac-toe technique that I fall for every time we play—it is vicious and I still can't figure it out. So hey, it is all about balance.

CHAPTER NINE

Be a joy vampire.

Since I became a mom, I have been able to take three small vacations without my kids. Once I went to a family wedding in Chicago with my sister, once a ladies' weekend at my friend's lake house, and once to a beachside retreat with my wild, wonderful coworkers where we did zero work and lots of celebrating. In all those instances, I quickly told the people I was sharing a room with that I had two rules: don't ask me for a snack, and don't wake me up in the middle of the night under any circumstance. If the hotel is on fire, maybe wake me up, but use your best judgment. Because that is what I wanted a break from the most—the endless cycle of my tiny offspring asking me for goldfish crackers, waking me up in the middle of the night by crawling into my bed, taking up 90 percent of my pillow space, and kicking me in the face with their tiny, sweet, dirty feet.

Sometimes, even in the middle of the night they ask me for a snack—the audacity. A one-two punch, waking me up and then asking for food. Parenting feels frustratingly repetitive and humdrum and sometimes like a lot and a little, all at once. It's beautiful, full of laughter and the most pure, sweet love I have ever known, of course. But also sometimes ... it's boring and monotonous, which makes me feel a little bit mom-guilty to say. But I know I am not the only one who feels this way, so I will say it loud and proud for the ones who need the solidarity. Haters can hate, but if it helps someone else to hear this, it is worth it for me. Sometimes, parenting just ain't fun. And I think that is normal.

If you are reading this and getting a little Judgy McJudgerson about my honesty, please know I am so, so grateful to be a mom and to have these two gorgeous babies. Especially with having a miscarriage, and now all we have gone through with Shepherd and his medical situation, the gift that my babies are is not lost on me.

But that isn't what this chapter is about. This is about the difficult times of parenting, so buckle up, Betty. I think that if we talk about these feelings more, we will feel less shame about them. If we normalize them, we can probably better handle them, right?

I have an amazing group of women at my church that I am very close with. We birthed babies alongside each other, created meal trains for each other in hard times, and have held massive clothing swaps.[1] One time, as we were driving to a lake house for that little ladies' weekend away, we stopped at a *very* rough-looking thrift store in the middle of nowhere—all of us fueled with the false hope that perhaps we would find some amazing,

---

[1]We didn't literally birth alongside each other, as in a physical sense. That would be weird. We all just had what seems like 9,035 babies among us over the past few years. Although honestly, it might make labor more fun if you go through it with a friend, right? We could make each other laugh between contractions and try to race to see who could get the baby out the fastest.

cheap vintage things to buy. Instead the *very* sketchy owner handed us bottles of water that likely were laced with drugs so he could kidnap us collectively as a unit. We politely accepted the water bottles, said thank you, didn't take a sip, and quickly browsed so it wouldn't look weird, and left. So, I would also like to think our friend group has been through a near-death experience together.

After we survived the creepy water-bottle-man incident, we went on to have a great weekend. We drank coffee out of little cups that said "rest and restore," sat by the water, read the Bible together, and walked the tiny downtown-area farmers' market. And as we all sat around that evening, talking and talking and talking—because ya know, a group of women at a lake house, that is what we do—something stood out to me. Every single woman there was offloading how difficult things were in parenting for them right now. Everyone was walking through a phase or season that was challenging them in one way or the other.

It wasn't in a "let's talk crap about our family and laugh about it" way, but they were just being honest about the struggles they were facing. Because hot dang, parenting is *hard*, for everyone. We forget this sometimes when we only get the highlight reels online of everyone's experience on social media. Until that moment of solidarity with these women, I had forgotten that we all walk through it. I had convinced myself I was the only one who was forever behind on laundry. Or that I was the only one who felt emotionally at my limit when dealing with the big feelings of my three-year-old, day after day. Good moms always have clean, folded laundry they immediately put away into drawers, and have never slammed down a jar of peanut butter in frustration, right? So . . . yeah. What does that make me?

I felt so sure that I was behind and failing. But in sharing all our experiences I realized that I was right where everyone else was—just trying to figure it all out and enjoy the ride as much as I can, even when it gets a little bananas. It helped me so much to hear about the mess of others. So, I will always contribute honestly as well, in hopes it might help someone else feeling like they are barely keeping their head above the water.

I think when we get into these ruts, these seasons of hard things and of sheer survival, one little thing to do to help get us out of the funk is to have a perspective shift.

Oh sorry—does that not sound exciting and life changing enough? *A mere perspective shift—that is the big idea here?* Boooooooring, as Shepherd would say.

Fine, Sally—I will change it to spice it up a bit. Don't simply have a shift in perspective. Instead, become a joy vampire. Yes, like Edward Cullen, but instead of sucking gross blood, you work to suck joy out of every little bit of your life, as much as possible, in order to survive.

We all know some times are easier than others. Some are harder, or lamer, sure. But if you really think about it—was life ever perfect? Like from the start of your adult life to now—was it? Gonna guess the answer is no.

Even before kids, Kyle and I were stressed about something—money, jobs, moving, grad school, whatever. But looking back with a bit of perspective on that season, I miss the slow weekends we had together, just the two of us. The time we spent hand in hand at random art festivals or taking short last-minute weekend getaways in a city we had never been to. We may have been stressed then about real-life things, but now I can also see the beauty that time had.

Because at the same time things might be difficult and stressful, there is so much beauty and joy to be sucked out of life. Even if it is in simple things, like toddler hugs, laughing with your spouse, a perfect sunrise, or a day at the beach where nobody gets stung by a jellyfish or sand up their nose.

I am only in my midthirties at this point, but looking back I can see some clear seasons of hard, and some clear seasons of ease, sure. But mostly, it all just blends together like one big life smoothie of good *and* bad times. That, in fact, is life. Life is now, today. Not four years from now when you *might* have enough money saved to go to Europe. Life also isn't ten years ago when you were thinner and tanner. Life is right now, and accepting that is a great step to fully enjoying it.

Right now I am in a season of snack slinging and managing the emotions of small humans, and my own emotions in the midst of all that. And while sometimes, it can feel a bit *blerg* and frustrating, it is also so sweet. I know that future me will look back and miss what it feels like to hold a three-year-old who is obsessed with snuggling my arm, even when I am really touched out for the day. I know that I will miss pausing whatever chore or task I needed to do because a sweet little girl asked me to play a game with her.

When I look back at my life and where I have come from, I mostly remember the good things. The good things are the ones that shine a bit brighter in my memories. And when we move forward to look back on our life now, we will likely do the same exact thing, especially when it comes to parenting. So let's enjoy them now, fully, before they become nothing but a memory.

I want to celebrate on a Tuesday night simply because it is Tuesday and I hate them, so why not make it fun? I want to stay up late with my friends dancing on the beach until 1:00 a.m. to music on an iPhone and not worry that I will be tired the next day. I want to remember exactly how my babies sounded and smelled and their sweet soft weight on me at this season of life. I want to remember their silly jokes that make no sense, their relentless love for me and stuffed animals, and how cute they look in their bright-colored swim goggles as they splash in the pool and say, "Mommy, watch!" over and over. I want to remember Kyle's first little tuft of gray hair, how handsome he looks when he chops down trees in our backyard, and how he still makes me laugh, even if it is only at 9:00 p.m. after the kids have (finally) gone to sleep.

It isn't always easy to find the little bits of joy in the midst of things that are hard. But life is flying by us, with every breath, with every sunset, with every goodnight kiss. The pandemic showed us all that. Shepherd's medical stuff has really driven that realization home for my family as well. If we don't take a hot minute to pause and actively look and fight for the goodness and joy that we are able to access right here and right now, we might miss it. Don't let the good stuff just become a memory. Breathe it all in today, even if in tiny bits. Savor it, enjoy it, as best as you can, as much as you can, as often as you can.

CHAPTER TEN

Stop placing all your hope for your family's future in Realtor.com.

When you are a youngish human being, your phone zone-out time likely is spent pursuing TikTok, Snapchat, Instagram, or Snoozel.[1] But something happens when you hit your late twenties and your thirties. Instead of ogling over the latest party photo dumps or the cutest new clunky dad sneakers, you are now gazing with jealousy and lust over homes for sale. That's right—where Instagram once used to be the apple of your eye, Realtor.com or Zillow has swept in and taken a solid place in your heart. If you know, you know.

I think that it isn't actually about the *house*, per se, but it is about dreaming of what kind of life you want to carve out for yourself, your spouse, your family. What do you want the next five, ten, thirty years to look like? You can't help but daydream about that stuff. Really thinking through what kind of childhood experience I wanted to give my kids is what sparked my real-estate obsession. Did I want them to be city high-rise dwellers

···

[1]Snoozel isn't a real thing. I made it up. But for a second did I make you feel old and out of touch? Teehee.

or run barefoot in the country?[2] I think striving for a life for your children that you can be proud of and feel good about is something every parent works toward in one way or another. Or just striving for a life *you* fully want.

Have you ever actually bought a house? The scrolling and searching can be a bit all-consuming. From the moment you even discuss starting to look, it can take up so much of your mental space. Because what if the day—hour!—that you don't check the neighborhood you are eyeing, something perfect gets listed and quickly snatched by someone else? Or you could be a few years from even having enough saved for a down payment, but you still spend your evenings looking at listings and wondering about what it would be like living here or there and seeing what pops up that would work for you and your family. For me, the looking, searching, waiting, hoping was draining on my brain and soul, like an unhealthy addiction to expired Halloween candy stashed in your freezer. Buying a home is something you try and control, but it really is one big process of trust and surrender. Because it can seem like the perfect home for you will never show up! Or that your situation—how much you can afford, where exactly you want to live—is near impossible. Or, you make five offers and they all get passed over for the cash asking price—I'm looking at you, 2022 real-estate market, you crazy girl.

Why am I even talking about this? Is this a low-key paid placement for Realtor.com?[3] No. I'm discussing it because

....

[2]I chose the barefoot in the country option. Watch out for the horse poop, kids, and I am sorry about the time you had to see a hawk eat one of our baby chickens. But maybe it builds character? Hard to say.

[3]Can paid placements become a thing in books? I will be the first one. Please start emailing me all your product samples and pitches. #sponsoredchapter

buying a house is a very tangible exercise in moving forward with hope, walking toward a goal or dream or something hard and overwhelming without having any real control or idea about how it will turn out.

Listen, it might not be about buying a home for you. That might not even be on your purview. Maybe it's establishing your career path or wanting to change it altogether and feeling like that is impossible. Or maybe it's searching for a spouse, or starting a family, or overcoming disease. Maybe it's trying to become the first person to ever free climb the Empire State Building in the nude—whatever your big, seemingly lofty goal is, insert it here.

For me, when I know with my whole heart and soul that I want something—like buying a home, having a child, or getting a certain job—thoughts of *Will this ever happen?* always creep in, those jerks. Drips of worry break through the dreams and cast doubt, even though I have seen God again and again make a way through what seemed impossible.

I have learned that trying to command your destiny is usually a failed attempt. At least it has been for me. Please promptly DM me if you have discovered a secret way to make everything work out exactly as you had planned. And I will need receipts.

I have seen, time and time again, that where you are going and will end up is something only God can ultimately make work out. No amount of Realtor.com scrolling and late-night searching and plotting and planning can 100 percent secure your path. And for some of you reading this, that might make you anxious, which I get. But also—perhaps it is refreshing? If we believe in a good God who loves us and cares about all the hairs on our heads—even the weird wiry gray ones that sprout up overnight and make you look like a witch—will he not take the reins, and bring you to a place that ultimately is best for you, for your life, your family, and his glory?

This isn't a prosperity gospel situation. Nah. I am not Joel Osteen, with hidden money in the bathroom walls, I promise. I am not saying that whatever we want in life we can get if we are just good enough and faithful enough. No way, man. I do believe God knows better than what we can plan for ourselves. What is best for you might not *be* buying that house that you think seems perfect. Or getting that job you were sure would have been amazing. I trust that God knows so much more than we ever could, so we can trust when these kinds of doors get shut.

But it can be hard to completely trust something to God's will that's such a huge chunk of your life—like finding an entire building to live in with your family that you can afford, that is safe, and that is near good schools, doesn't have a secret rat infestation, or isn't low-key haunted. It's all a lot.

When our family first moved back to Florida, Sunny wasn't even two yet and Shepherd was just a "one day" hope and dream. The house we first bought was something we could afford, which at the time, in Florida, meant it was also in a neighborhood where people left plywood up on their windows for about a year after a hurricane passed through, just because it was a lot of work to take it down and the homeowners association didn't care. We loved our little house, but Sunny only had a cramped street lined with cars to run around and play on, and one time a person walked by and dumped an entire black trash bag of junk in my yard. I yelled at her and it got awkward. Trash dumping aside, Kyle and I wanted something with a bit more room, a bit more nature. We maybe even wanted our own swimming pool, not just the community one that closed one day because we had a serial pool poop offender, who the home-owners association made a very clear point to let us know was a full-grown adult, not even just a teen making a bad joke. An adult. The same one, every time. Lord, have mercy on us all.

So after living in our first house for three years without ever once going in the community pool, and then having Shepherd, we were ready for more space.

We knew where we wanted to be—out in a neighborhood called the Acreage where each plot was . . . you guessed it . . . an acre. People owned farm animals for fun out there, and teens rode their horses bareback down the street while texting their friends.[4] And, it was only about a thirty-minute drive away from the beach, so yeah. It all felt surreal and magical and the perfect amount of country and island vibe that one could want in Florida. But it seemed *impossible*, even though we knew in our heart this was where we wanted to be. Kyle and I were neck deep in our Realtor.com scrolling obsession and would drive through the neighborhood looking for available plots of land or For Sale signs and just wonder if it could ever actually happen for us. It's hard for something so big and potentially life changing to not occupy so much of your mental space.

Kyle and I were talking one day, and we both felt in our heart that something would just pop up and move forward quickly,

---

[4]This really does happen, and I will never get over it. Teens, never with saddles—I don't know why, maybe saddles are not cool—riding down the street on their horses, texting their friends they are on their way. I feel like this is a great way to raise kids. Would it be better if they were not on their phones while riding a horse? Yes, but we will take what we can get.

but we had zero idea how. Isn't that how good things come mostly? They are not there until one day they *are*. The yes. The home. The positive pregnancy test. Finding love. It's just the waiting and the having hope part that can be kinda hard.

After a few months of searching, a new listing popped up. The pictures were grainy and didn't look very professional, but we thought it had potential. Kyle decided to drive by on his way back from work, and he instantly loved it. The next day he drove me past, and I also instantly loved it. All we had seen was the outside that needed . . . a lot of work. But we just, well, loved it.

The owner was a realtor and was selling it all by herself. She decided to do just one day of showings—on Halloween. This is a very strange day to choose to show a house, but I feel like in a way it weeded out any buyers who weren't serious. If you had a higher priority of perfecting your *Stranger Things* costume that morning, then this wasn't the house for you.

We showed up right when the open house began and were the only ones there the entire time. The owner walked us around the property and told us everything and anything we would need to know, as if we had already purchased it. Kyle and I just looked at each other in that way only a married couple can and said silently with our eyes—*this was the place*. It was random, a bit quirky, it made no sense, but it felt perfect for us. That evening we made an offer, she accepted, and with a few bumps along the closing process way, we suddenly owned a big white house with a front and back porch, and a barn that I would immediately work to fill with pointless yet cute farm animals.[5]

....

[5] The "bump" was that a former owner of the house put a metal roof on all by himself . . . right over the shingle roof, actually. And did he permit it? Nope. Old men who install their own metal roofs do not believe in

So many things since then have worked out better than we had imagined. Kyle ended up getting a new job that was even closer to our new house, which was a plus. The seller, when she found out I was an author, burst into tears because her sister who had recently passed away was also a writer. And a woman named Meli moved in next door the same week we did, and we quickly became the best of friends. So it all just worked out, and I can only attribute it to God. Because a new friend, a better commute, and comforting someone who recently lost a loved one wasn't a box I checked during my online searches. All of those things that felt so special and specific to us did not come from the Realtor.com corporate office—if it did, that would be very creepy. It was more than that. It was spiritual and intentional and very surprising. And I think we can allow room for that in our lives. Pray, trust, and let God do the rest.

I do believe that in the way buying this house worked out for us, something can work out for you too. Whatever you are trusting God with right now, home buying and beyond, there is a possibility that it could turn out better than you could have planned for you and your family, better than you could have imagined, really.

And it has to be said that it might not turn out in the exact way you plan or hope for. But I do believe that if we trust the path that God has for our life, it will be the best path.

If you are facing something that seems like an impossible mountain right now, I pray that you will keep your eyes looking up. Keep them off the junk that could possibly get in your way

---

permits, obviously. So insurance just thought the home had a thirty-year-old shingle roof and wouldn't insure the house because of that. No worries, we got a new roof eventually but MY GOODNESS the drama.

and up toward the hope. I pray that you can fixate on that hope that comes from a God who loves you and cares, and your joy will remain present even as you face the unknown. From buying a house, to facing an illness, to looking for the love of your life— it isn't easy, I know. I never want to gloss over those very real and sometimes difficult feelings.

With each challenge I face, I really try to fight to keep hope in the center of my line of sight. Does it take regular reminders? Yes. But I continue to fight to keep the joy in the midst of the hardship, even when it takes a bit of extra effort. Together, we can take the big, scary steps toward the desires of our heart, and ask (or annoyingly beg, if you are anything like me) God to carry us along the way.

I had a client once, a beautiful writer named Margaret Dulaney, who wrote something in an article I will never forget: "Cynicism is a lazy slide down a slippery slope on a flabby ass. Hope, on the other hand, hope requires that you engage the old gluteus maximus, and stand up. In short, hope requires courage, where cynicism requires absolutely nothing."[6]

First, I mostly loved that this sweet, soft-spoken, gorgeous literary writer wrote "flabby ass" in a way that was so profound. But also, this quote was such a fresh perspective I needed.

It isn't easy to simply have hope. It is easy to be cynical though. Whoops—guilty as charged. But if we acknowledge and re-member that having hope isn't always the easiest choice but definitely the best choice, we can continue to fight hard for it and not be surprised if it takes a bit of work.

....

[6]Another serious footnote! Margaret Dulaney, "Finding Hope in Dark Times," World Religion News, November 4, 2020, www.worldreligion news.com/issues/finding-hope-dark-times-margaret-dulaney.

I think sometimes we expect that having assured hope is a natural response to the faith in the Lord that is woven so deeply into our hearts. I wish it were the case! But it isn't. Hope requires focus. Intentionality. It requires strength and action, choosing to remain hopeful, to have faith even when you don't know the outcome of the big, scary thing you are up against.

I do think that your hope muscle can grow stronger with time too. Like a bulging spray-tanned bicep on the cringiest of bodybuilding competitors—maybe that is the level of strength we can aim for. With each test, with each new season, maybe our hope muscle can continue to grow—no steroids or chalky protein shakes required. So, let's get off our flabby butts and have hope, as best we can, and trust God along the way.

PART 4

Don't talk about my best friend like that; a.k.a. be kind to yourself, boo.

ONE THING THAT I LEARNED from the pandemic, and from walking through other long and difficult seasons, is that sometimes you just need to pause and be kind to yourself. Seems cheap and easy to say, I know. But it is also important. We so often are quick to pour kindness onto others—which we should, duh. Our spouses, our kids, our clients, our siblings and parents and friends—anybody in our little circle. But when it comes to ourselves, it feels weird and almost excessive to take a minute to pause, breathe, and do something kind for ourselves when things are feeling extra rough.

The older I get the less tolerance I have for rudeness—including my own rudeness toward myself.

Recently I made a new best friend—that next-door neighbor, Meli, who moved in the same week we did to our new house. At the ripe ol' age of thirty-five it is still possible to make a new friend, apparently. And yes, we do act like we are twelve and wear as many matching outfits as possible, if you must know. We didn't know each other in middle school, so we have to make up for lost time in all ways possible. The point is—whenever I say something self-deprecating about myself, she says, "Don't talk about my best friend like that." It is such a good reminder to be kind in the way we think and talk about ourselves, and of course treat ourselves.

I hope that just as much as you can recognize the stress and strife that pops up, you can recognize the need for a little bit of self-kindness. A morning spent in Scripture. A night tucked in early with a good book. Filling your house with worship music or screamo music and just letting it all go for a minute. Exercising. Spending time with a friend who makes you laugh. Taking a day to hide under your covers and nap for hours like an old, dying cat—sometimes you need that also. For me, I am just trying to recognize the bad feelings more, and then try to take care of them kindly instead of ignoring them or trying to just push through. I am just trying to be a bit kinder to myself, because for goodness' sake I have been through a lot. And so have you.

CHAPTER ELEVEN

Make friends with a firefighter who buys matching muumuus at Walmart with you.

Okay, so about that friend I wear matching outfits with. Just a couple days after my family moved into our new home, she walked up to the fence and introduced herself as my neighbor, Meli. She had just moved in that past week as well with her boyfriend, so we were both neighborhood newbies. She had blond hair, a really cute outfit, perfect nails, and a big smile. We were chatting through all the basics of what you discuss with someone the first time you meet. Naturally, the question of "What do you do?" came up, and she told me she was a firefighter.

For about two seconds, I was very confused. I was like, *Wait, what? You?* And then my brain actually woke up from being ridiculous and just thinking that firefighters are only men with beer bellies or young hotties that one day will become old men with beer bellies. This lady in cutoff jean shorts and perfect pink nails was the one who was literally paid to run into burning buildings and carry humans out. GET IT QUEEN! I then told her I sit in front of a computer and write

words for a living so . . . yeah. Not as exciting as the burning-
building, lifesaving stuff. Despite the difference in our careers,
we clicked. We exchanged numbers and I walked away excited
that I was going to maybe have a friendly face next door who
could also provide immediate EMT services if needed—what
a bonus!

Over the next few weeks Meli and I would text a bit about
random neighborly things, and talk at the fence when we saw
each other in passing. The texts turned from more formal next-
door-neighbor things like, "Did you see that crazy dog who ate
my chicken is running down the street again?" to funny TikToks
and memes, which I knew meant it was official—Meli and I
were real friends. Neighbors *and* friends—perhaps the best
combination. You know when you are in middle school and plan
with all your buds to buy houses next to each other when you
are old? I was now doing that. I just happened to meet my bud
when I was in my thirties.

For the first few months, secretly I was really searching for a
sort of red flag to emerge because we were just getting along so
well. Like what are the odds you move next door to someone
you actually like seeing every day? I was waiting for Meli to say
something super off-putting, like she hated cheese and champagne or was going to start breeding pythons in her backyard—
but she didn't.[1] We were so different, yet so similar in all the
ways that matter in friendships. We had the same sense of
humor and were both extremely social to the point we weird
people out at the grocery store when we eagerly talk to them.

....

[1]Honestly, I could see her doing the python thing, but at this point our
  friendship runs deep, so it wouldn't even be a deal breaker. I would probably purchase her pythons cute hats to wear, that is how much I love her.

And we both love to text funny, dumb things, which I feel is an esteemed quality in a friend. We like to be outside with animals and country things, which is good because we both basically live on farms. But we also like to get our nails done as much as humanly possible, and we will never turn down a Starbucks.

One night Kyle and I saw Meli and her boyfriend, Ricky, were having a bonfire. Meli and Ricky's fire pit sits right next to our fence, so we walked over to say hi and quickly chat. It was then that Meli actually *did* say something weird. "Do you like murder?" she asked.

In most circumstances, that would be a huge red flag. But lucky for her, that is just my flavor of weird because, yes, I love murder! But what she meant by "murder" is true crime shows. These dark documentaries are one of my biggest guilty pleasures, and now I had a friend to share them with. So yes, Meli, I love murder, but perhaps next time say "murder shows" for clarity's sake.

The more Meli and I hung out, the closer we became. We blared our favorite high school punk bands for each other as we drove down our road for our quarterly Walmart shopping sprees.[2] We bought matching overalls and muumuus and rhinestone sunglasses, and we wore them proudly. We met regularly at the fence to cry and laugh after hard days, and we tried out all the latest TikTok makeup and health trends together with shared optimism.

....

[2] I realize how backwoods country this sentence sounds, but we actually live about twenty minutes from a big downtown city. We just choose to live on a dirt road because we think it's awesome, and while Target is a tiny bit closer, we actually prefer Walmart. I LIKE THEIR CLOTHES BETTER. THERE I SAID IT. And I am cheap, so . . . Walmart.

Luckily, Meli was equally as obsessed with farm animals as Kyle and I were. And I say *luckily* because our pasture butts right up to her fence, so she basically inherited a petting zoo as well. As Kyle and I built our hobby farm out—first chickens, then a senior pony, then three goats, then two pigs, then more chickens and a turkey named Bob who is obsessed with me—Meli was equally as excited as I was every time we brought home our new fuzzy bundle of joy. She was with me when the vet did a field neuter surgery in my backyard (what is my life?) for my favorite goat, Clifford, and I was horrified. With fascination, Meli watched the vet slice and dice, because a goat neuter is nothing in comparison to what she has seen on her job, and I hid behind her in fear. I, in turn, forced her to dust off the dirt road, trade in boots for heels and showed her the ropes of downtown West Palm Beach on a girls' night out. We balance each other out.

Then, one day, she called me her bestie. WE WERE NOW BEST FRIENDS. Who gets a new best friend in their thirties?! It was such a beautiful, unexpected, but oh-so-needed gift from the Lord. I really do believe it. God can drop amazing people in your life at any moment, and at any age, and I think it is important to remember that. For me, being the most extroverted human on the planet with a very introverted husband, I need friends. And now, one of my closest friends happened to live next door.

But this chapter isn't just about our friendship—that is just necessary background information. It is about her strength.

Meli, as I said, is a firefighter and a paramedic. She runs straight into danger and takes quick action, while I hide at the sight of a little goat blood. She is the first on the scene of accidents and fires and heart attacks and shootings and the worst moments of people's lives, ready to dive right in and do whatever has to be done. She is so strong in so many areas of her life. She kicks butt at work, crushes it at the gym, and is such a supportive friend and girlfriend, dog owner and plant aficionado. But also she is real about where she's struggling, and we've had some deep, honest conversations because nobody is a complete robot superhero. Her mental strength and fight are fierce all across the map, and I wanted that for myself.

When I met Meli, I didn't feel like I was at my strongest, by any means. Before we moved, our family had been through a very hard season with Shepherd's medical stuff. And, after a few months break, I knew we needed to dive back in. We were gearing up for a fresh round of appointments and checkups and tests, and I really, really didn't want to do it. I didn't want my baby to have to go through that again. But I knew that soon enough I would be back on the phone, listening to the hospital on-hold music of my nightmares while I waited an hour to schedule a test for my son that I was terrified of but knew he needed. I would soon have to look at my calendar and space out his visits to make sure he was only facing one awful procedure a month to alleviate his medical trauma, or try to group up as many appointments as needed in Miami all on one day so we didn't have to make the two-hour drive there over and over again. I was so tired of waiting on a doctor to walk in and talk through scary test results, my stomach feeling like it was doing backflips worthy of an Olympic gold medal. I was so tired of holding down my son while he got poked and tested. I didn't want to do all the scary, awful, heartbreaking, hard stuff again. Of course, I would for my child, but I sure as heck didn't want to, and I was fighting against accepting it was time.

So, as I began that process of gearing our family up for our new wave of medical madness, I wanted more mental strength to face whatever outcome we got for Shepherd. Whatever his specialists said about his sweet special body, how things were progressing or not, I wanted to be able to stand strong for him. I wanted the same amount of emotional strength it took to run into blazing fires and fight to save people's lives, except I would use that strength to care for my son and our family well.

I was tired of being scared. I was tired of being wrapped in anxiety as we walked through the weeks of appointments and waiting to hear about results. I was tired of my brain being consumed by the fear that seeing each of Shepherd's specialists brought about, thinking about what they might say, what we might need to do next. I wanted to be stronger, not only for my mental health but for Shepherd's. He was getting older and was more aware of what was happening. He was so brave himself— never fussing over a test, not even a shot. Having grown up seeing multiple doctors all throughout the year, he thinks it is normal. He likes the blood pressure test even—he says it feels like his arm is getting a hug, bless him. And it was Shepherd, anyway—not me—who was getting the tests done, having to sit in the scary machines, having to be pumped with radiation or anesthesia and be x-rayed to no avail. He was the one doing the *really* hard stuff. So, I was ready to become stronger for him. And for myself.

When she wanted to share, Meli told me some of the tough things she had to do on her shifts. Some of these things she told me—I couldn't even begin to imagine what it would be like to experience that. But for her it was just another day on the job, and she would come home, recover, and then do it all over again.

That is the kind of strength I wanted. I wanted the ability to face whatever scary thing is in front of me with the emotional aptitude of an old rhino who no longer gives a crap about anything. Strong, stoic, calm, slow and steady, but super ready to charge and attack at any moment if needed. An old rhino who gives zero craps. It's the perfect analogy.

I wanted to gear up and run toward each appointment like I was running toward a car or fire and ready to kick its butt. And I felt my firefighter friend could teach me how to do that, if only by osmosis. Because I really do feel the people you surround yourself with matter. And Meli emulated strength, positivity, joy, and a fierce don't-mess-with-me attitude. I needed all of that in my own life.

One day we were chatting, driving down the dirt road with the music blaring to go "into town" as I like to call it—a.k.a. a fifteen-minute drive out of our horse-laden neighborhood back to reality. We were on a mission for a Dunkin' and some new press-on nails at CVS when she mentioned something firefighters are taught to do as they approach a burning structure, and it really stuck with me.

Try before you pry.

For a firefighter, what this means is, in the excitement of coming up to a structure on fire, just try the door first to see if it's unlocked before kicking or axing it in. Try the *easy thing first* because hey—it might work out just fine doing it that way. No axe required.

This is so simple but also so applicable to our lives. Yes, we might not be running toward a burning building. But how often, when something challenging is in front of us, do we immediately jump to the worst-case scenarios in our minds? How often do we worry and freak out, instead of just doing the simple things first? Like praying. Then praying again. Then focusing on the good, easy things that could happen, because they are also a possibility.

Maybe the doctors will give you good test results. Maybe you will get the house, or the job, or the one yes from someone that you need. Maybe your eighty-ninth blind date will be the one where you finally meet the love of your life.

How often do we flip out and try to axe down a door all on our own when God might be right there to easily open it up for us if we let him? Try before you pry.

When Meli told me about this concept—although again, she was literally talking about a house on fire—I thought, *Hmm. Maybe . . .* maybe *. . . I could do that but in my life.* Maybe I could go to Shepherd's specialist appointments with a sense of calm and simply see how they unfolded. Because maybe they would go okay. Heck, maybe they would even go more than okay! Maybe we would get great results, or a good diagnosis, or a little mini miracle. Maybe the door was going to be open for us easily, and there was no need to whip out my emotional battle-axe to have a Jack Nicholson in *The Shining* moment after all.

Maybe you can walk toward your own scary thing with a try-before-you-pry mentality too. Be kind to yourself, give yourself space to feel all your feelings, but then just freaking try. See how things go before falling apart with worry, anxiety, and stress. Because maybe the door is going to be unlocked after all.

Being around Meli, seeing her love of life and her bravery in the face of some of the worst situations a human being could ever face, made me feel stronger about facing my own battles. Just through our friendship, she taught me how to be stronger emotionally and physically—I learned simply by hearing her stories and seeing how she approached really scary stuff both on the job and in her daily life.

And I needed that. I needed to soak up the energy of someone who was completely ready to run headfirst into danger without batting an eye. I wanted to stand firm. To face whatever I had to face ahead.

I now knew that what we were working through with Shepherd wasn't "curable" or something that would go away. The whole nature of VACTERL is you just handle each body issue one by one when it becomes a problem. It really is the ultimate test of parental endurance—working through all the body parts, at different ages and stages of his life. Monitoring and watching and praying and hoping things stay healthy, but being prepared if they do not.

I was ready to be stronger for my son and for myself. I was ready to accept that my job was to fight for him forever. Beyond that, I was ready to start advocating and helping others on their own medical journey or whatever other challenge they were facing. I am not the only one with a sick child, not the only one who has a child with a disability or a difference, clearly. I was ready to stand a bit firmer for Shepherd, and for anyone else who might need a little encouragement as well along the way.

And learning to try before I pry—or just approach a scary thing with a sense of calm and hope—was a great step in the right direction for that.

But it wasn't just emotional strength I needed. In my heart I knew I needed to level up in all areas of my life—spiritually, emotionally, but also physically. I knew that if I channeled my angst and anger into getting physically stronger, I would be emotionally stronger along the way.

So, guess what Meli and I did? We became Rocky Balboa. Because what better thing can you do in hard times than become a sweaty, punching man with a thick Philadelphia accent and a perfect vintage sweatsuit collection? It just feels like the best choice. We got Sylvester Stallone wigs, 1980s-style hoodies and pants, and bright red boxing gloves and began to wear them all around our neighborhood to conjure up big Rocky energy in our lives.

Just kidding. That would be super weird. We are strange but have yet to dip into that level of costume-wearing strange. We just joined a boxing gym, and we certainly did not wear a wig at any point because that would be itchy.

Also, for the record, Meli is very scared of bees. So when we are on a walk or chatting at the fence and one approaches, it is my turn to be the hero. But let's talk more about boxing. *Bzz.*

CHAPTER TWELVE

Punch something hard until you feel better. Preferably not a human, however.

A few months into my friendship with Meli, she invited me to go try this new boxing studio that opened up close by. When she asked me to go with her, I had zero excuses to say no. Trust me—I tried to think of one because exercise is, well, exercise. But I knew I needed some sort of change. I wanted to get stronger physically and emotionally, and apparently punching things was the way I was going to do that.

When we walked into the little studio that first day, the trainer began asking us initial questions about our physical state. "How much do you exercise?" "What level of fitness are you at?" All the things that make you take a cold hard look at how little you have done physically. So I told him the truth!

"All you need to know," I said, "is that the most exercise I have done in the last three years was giving birth to a human being."

Meli laughed and the dude squirmed a bit as he tried to respond to my honest-yet-awkward statement, and we moved right along. But it was true—giving birth and chasing around a toddler was about as active as I had gotten.

He got us our boxing gloves. They were straight up big ol' mittens like any grown boxing human man would use, and I loved it. He taught us how to wrap up our hands like little burritos so we wouldn't hurt our fingers when we were annihilating a punching bag like it was trying to steal our purses. And that was it! With our wrapped hands and our big manly gloves that made us look like Knuckles from Sonic the Hedgehog, Meli and I began the first class. We moved from station to station, hitting and kicking and doing burpees, lifting weights and just basically working out every single muscle possible in our bodies. It was so hard but felt amazing.

Afterward—Starbucks in hand because it was conveniently placed right next to the gym and we will never say no to a Starbies—Meli and I felt like we could take on the universe. Our bodies were pumped full of caffeine and endorphins, I had my friend next to me, we were blaring Lizzo, and it was perfect. We knew we were hooked. So with that, we became boxers. Well, sort of. We became gals who were obsessed with our boxing gym and the Starbucks run afterward, and that was good enough for me.

The more that we went to the boxing gym, the more I realized it wasn't just the cardio and weights that I needed—it was the actual act of hitting things. When I was going ham on the punching bag, anger bubbled up from deep inside that I didn't even realize I had squished down and had been carrying with me. I was mad. I was mad that Shepherd had to go through all the doctor appointments and tests. I was mad that things didn't turn out like I would've planned for my son. I was even, apparently, mad at jerk nurses and doctors we had encountered early on who treated us with flippancy during a deeply vulnerable, emotional time. Dumb stuff people said or faces that had caused my pain popped up. People and things I hadn't thought of in months, a year even. I realized it wasn't all "fine" like I had said far too many times. So often in my perpetual quest for optimism I brush things off without ever fully processing them, to a point where it becomes unhealthy. Punching apparently unearths those things from the depths of my soul—things I didn't even know I was carrying around. But, man, it felt good to unload them. I can see now that I was completing my body's stress cycle. Well, actually more like one hundred little stress cycles from one hundred stressful things that had happened over the past few years that I never really wrapped up in a healthy way.

One day, as Meli and I showed up at our little gym, she knew that I was in a really bad place that day. I had spent the entire car ride over talking about how I was so, so sick of trying to set up this sedated MRI with a hospital that had the most frustrating booking system. I was spending hours trying to make an appointment for my child, and then getting referrals and clearances and all the things required from constantly cranky office receptionists. It all felt like some weird parental torture laced with bad phone waiting music. And it was all so I could do something I really, really didn't want to have to do—again. We did it once when Shepherd was just a tiny baby, and it was one of the scariest days of my life. Now we were gearing up to do it all over, with an older, more aware child. I so badly didn't want to have to hand my sweet baby over to an anesthesiologist to be taken away from me for hours while Kyle and I just sat, waiting and staring at a wall until we could be with him again. I hated the whole process, and I was so mad that it was again a part of our life and our story, and I just wanted it to not be.

So, that day when we started our workout circuit and I got to the big punching bag, I punched with so much gusto that I think I scared the trainer. The dude gave me a look like, *dang girl, are you okay?* And then he told me to just keep punching. He said forget about the set we were working on and just punch in any way or form that I could, as hard as I could. So I did. I punched and punched and punched until it felt like my little arms would fall off, and then I punched some more. I punched so hard that the massive weighted bag split and fell to the ground in defeat.

Okay fine, the bag-splitting thing actually didn't happen, but it would have been a really exciting story to tell. The bag stayed put, despite the murderous rage I unleashed on it—remember how I was new at this whole working out thing?

When I was finally done punching and punching and punching, I didn't realize how much I needed it. I needed to just get all my bad, icky emotions out in a very physical way. Things were not fine. They just weren't, and I desperately wanted to not feel any more bad feelings. The cheap Band-Aids of "it's going to be okay" were starting to peel off because there was real physical stress, fear, and trauma beneath them. Something about the actual act of punching helped me to release all that anger that had been sitting dormant in my gut the past few years, and especially the anger then as I geared up for more tests, more procedures, more fear for my child.

I think now, I realize, that as much as I don't want to feel big bad feelings, if I don't let them out and process them in a healthy way, they just harden and weigh me down. It wasn't until I punched the daylights out of a bag that I realized the emotions were even there in the first place, rotting. I know now that you have to let that stuff out—through punching, taking a moment to fully cry or grieve, therapy, blaring metal music, whatever. But it has to come out if you want to get stronger.

Now guys—punching a big, heavy punching bag is pretty straightforward. You take your fist and hit a massive object that barely quivers in return, and it feels great. Fist hits the bag, repeat. But you know those little dangling speed bags that boxers in movies punch again and again with lightning precision? The gym also had one of those, and we would always wrap up the class with a turn at that darn speed bag, and I quickly realized that it was not an easy thing. You would think such a small object wouldn't be such a big issue, but such is life, right?

The first time I tried the speed bag, I looked like a cat who had way too much catnip and was trying to catch a fly—paws up, clumsily waving around in the air, moving way too slow, and not really connecting with anything substantial. It was embarrassing. Who knew that such a tiny punching bag would be one of the most challenging things to get a grasp on? It wasn't physically hard, but it was mentally hard. You really, really had to focus, which is never my strong point to begin with.

I kept at it, class after class. Eventually, I stopped looking like a stoned kitten and closer and closer to someone who Sylvester Stallone would slightly approve of. And one day, while I was punching at a steady pace—right hand, left hand, right hand, left hand—it hit me. Not the bag but a realization. The most important thing to mastering that speed bag was keeping up the rhythm. If you hesitate, second-guess yourself, or shy away from going all in, it throws the whole process off. You have to keep moving, even if you are not exactly sure where your punch will land. You have to keep up the momentum or else you will get off track. You have to keep going.

I realized that with Shepherd's medical journey, I had lost the momentum. I was just trying to avoid, hide, or numb out from the scary things instead of facing them. I got out of rhythm, and stepping back in now, as we were going to head back to the hospital for another fully sedated MRI and a meeting with the neurosurgeon to discuss if he needed surgery, felt scary and overwhelming. I felt weak and unstable. But through the little speed bag dingle dangle thing, I felt God saying to me that I needed to get back in the rhythm. I needed to get back into the practice of facing the hard things right away, feeling the feelings, grieving the little griefs, and continuing to fight forward anyway for my child and myself. I had to gear up, go all in, and show up with full strength. I had to keep punching, again and again, even if I didn't know what the outcome would really be or how the punches would exactly land.

There in my gym with the little awkward punching bag, I decided I was going to get back into the rhythm of my life until it became easier and easier to make the hard hits. I knew that I needed to show up with full strength and not hesitate if I was going to defeat this big scary thing and not let it defeat me back in the process. I also knew that God would be there with me the entire way, like a boxing coach in the corner of my ring with a thick Philly accent, a crooked little hat on his head, wiping my blood and sweat and encouraging me to get back in the fight and swing harder.

When I started boxing, I never thought I would learn such strange deep life lessons, or that I would release so much sup-pressed anger that had been hiding beneath my weak attempts at remaining positive or my ability to just distract myself from fully feeling the feelings. I realized that to be strong, I needed to slow down, dig deep, and feel the bad stuff fully until it didn't hurt as much anymore. I needed to do that so I could stand upright and kick the crap out of whatever opponent I was facing that day, one punch at a time.

I know you might not want to go to a sweaty boxing gym. I get it. But is there something else that you can tap into to release whatever needs to be let free from your tightly clenched chest? To complete your stress cycles so you can heal, you can breathe, you can move forward a little stronger? It could be a hike in nature. A solid weekend of laughing with your best friend over charcutes. A therapist who forces you to face whatever it is you are trying to avoid. Whatever you need to do. Punch it out. Close it up. Heal. I want that for you.

CHAPTER THIRTEEN

······································

Write an anti-love letter.
It's okay.

Something else happened when I was punching things like a professional boxer on his best and worst day. As I hit hard and let my aggression out in such a physical way, it came to the surface just exactly what was *causing* it in the first place. Sure, there were the obvious things: the pandemic, general parenting stress, anger over what Shepherd had to go through and what Kyle and I had to go through as parents, and the scary upcoming appointments. But often, when I was punching, the same *person* would come to my mind, again and again. Someone I didn't even realize I was holding on to such anger for. Gasp! I know. The scandal.

As a follower of Jesus, I recognize forgiveness is everything. Of course. Everyone needs so much grace as we walk through this life—me especially. But I realized that I hid behind this a bit more than was probably healthy. "Hid behind" meaning I was quick to brush over things, say, "it's fine, we're all a mess," and try to just move on when people hurt me, without processing or acknowledging what actually happened.

But just pretending I wasn't hurt or angry and shoving the emotions deep down until they were eating at my soul—was that really forgiving anyway? Seemed to me it was more like ignoring and suppressing. I knew I needed to process my feelings, and then I needed to let them go.

Everyone in my personal circle who is reading this right now is probably like, *Oh gosh was she thinking about me in anger when punching away at a punching bag?* Well, I wasn't. If I were thinking about you, you would have received an anti-love letter from me. Let me explain.

I was thinking about a medical assistant. Anticlimactic, right? But when punching out my emotions, I continued to think about her—a random woman we met at one of Shepherd's very first specialist appointments. Kyle and I were freshly trying to figure out what was happening with our tiny six-month-old baby. Up until then, we had only known about his heart defect, which we assumed was mostly under control at that point.

As I mentioned in chapter three, once Shepherd started sitting up, he was extremely crooked and his head and back seemed to lean to one side. Kyle and I thought, *Perhaps a simple case of torticollis*, which could be fixed with physical therapy. So we went to the pediatric orthopedic surgeon to figure out next steps.

Once they took an x-ray the orthopedic surgeon came in with his medical assistant in tow. The surgeon then quickly and dismissively rattled off all of the things he found wrong with my sweet baby. Guys, as you know, it was not torticollis. Nothing muscular actually, but instead a large handful of potentially very serious birth defects on major organs and bones. Cool cool. My head started spinning as the surgeon said terms I had never even heard of. He told us we needed to go to a children's hospital and

get him a sedated MRI as a next step so they could really un-
cover what was wrong with him. Then he quickly left the room
before we even knew what questions to ask.

I was in shock, trying to process what the surgeon had said.
He had delivered life-altering news in such a short and flippant
way, then quickly shut the door and loudly asked his team,
"Who wants to order Jimmy John's?" before cracking jokes in
the hallway right outside the door with his assistant. All this
while Kyle and I tried to pack up Shepherd into his car seat and
function as normal human beings without melting into a puddle
of despair.

We went home, and I was still confused about what had just
happened. I knew we needed to get the MRI, but that is such a
huge thing to do for a little baby. It would be at the children's
hospital and Shepherd would undergo full anesthesia, which is
scary even as an adult. I would do whatever needed to be done
for my son, of course, but I didn't fully understand *why* it was
needed. After thinking and sorting through my thoughts for a
few days, I finally had tangible follow-up questions to ask before
I felt comfortable enough moving forward.

I called the office and tried to get another appointment
with the orthopedic surgeon to continue our conversation,
but they didn't feel it was necessary. I asked if he was willing
to have a quick phone call and talk through some things with
me, but he wouldn't do that either. But I had to talk to
someone before I did the MRI with any amount of peace. I
had questions.

After leaving another desperate message to the office line
trying to get more answers, I finally was called back by the doctor's medical assistant—the one I kept thinking about while

punching things at the gym a year later. She said to me, "Listen, I have been working in this field for twenty years. Do you want me to just talk you through everything?"

As a seasoned medical parent, I now know the next thing to ask is, "Are you a nurse or a doctor?" If they are not, ask to speak with one instead. Because girlfriend wasn't any of that. She was responsible for booking appointments and taking notes, which is an important part of the field, but she should not have been dispensing medical advice. But apparently, she had enough confidence to talk me through what the heck she *thought* was happening with my child.

What she told me was my son had spina bifida occulta, and his spine bones were not fully developed.

This sounds absolutely horrifying for a variety of reasons, and googling sure didn't help the matter. But that is what she told me he had, and she said that it was very important we do the MRI, and that was that.

For two months while we waited for the MRI day to come—the soonest they could get us in—all I was thinking about was my son's spine was not formed fully, that he had spina bifida occulta, and that he might never walk. For *two whole months* that is what I was fixated on, which is about eight hundred thousand times longer than any parent should have to worry about their child.

Guys, he doesn't have spina bifida occulta. Every specialist we've seen since then looks at me so confused when I ask about it, and then says spina bifida occulta is not anything to worry about at all. Yet this lady on the phone, who never went to medical school, decided to tell me my son's spine wasn't fully formed and that it was a big deal, and then hang up and probably go order more Jimmy John's and crack more office jokes.

I now know how wrong she was. And how wrong it was for her to even try and diagnose my son without the credentials to do so.

I also now realize how much I was holding on to anger about that. Normally, I don't hold grudges. But I think there is a difference between holding a grudge and feeling real, genuine hurt about something for a justifiable reason. I was mad. I felt wronged, and my soul was apparently not going to settle the heck down until I dealt with it.

So, it was that lady who kept popping into my brain whenever I was in full Rocky punching mode, and frankly I was tired of thinking about her. I should have been punching away anger over a sassy client email or a silly nothing fight with Kyle, but I kept going back to this person who I only met once and spoke briefly to on the phone a week later, but who caused me months of extreme heartache and anxiety. I remember bawling at church one day during worship shortly after my conversation with her, just wondering if my son would ever be able to walk, to grow, to be okay.

As I punched and she kept coming into my mind, I realized first, how deeply that season had hurt me. Sometimes you don't realize how affected you are by things until you are months or years away and finally able to let down and process. Also, I was so tired of thinking about it. I was too worn down from everything else happening in life to carry that old weight, and I wanted it to be released.

But how? How do you release it? Simply punching a bag clearly wasn't enough—it just brought to the forefront of my brain the anger I had shoved down so deep and pretended didn't exist. I needed something more. Punching the actual person? Nah. Getting arrested sounded exhausting.

So, I wrote a letter. A strongly worded letter—gasp! Going against all my Midwestern-niceness instincts, I wrote to her. Not a mean letter, but a letter that was straightforward, to the point, and expressed things that are not necessarily shiny or pretty yet still so desperately needed to be said.

In my anti-love letter, as I like to call it, I cut right to the chase and offloaded the pain and hurt she caused me with her careless words. And that the way she and the doctor had acted toward us, parents at a very stressful and life-changing moment, was simply cold. I told her all the misinformation she told me over the phone—that she casually spouted out diagnoses for my baby that were awful and simply not true. And because of that, for months, I had to worry about those diagnoses. I told her that after her phone call I wasn't even sure if my son would be able to walk, and I had ruminated over that fear until eventually he did walk a half a year later. I urged her to treat suffering parents better in the future.

And then I deleted the letter and simply felt better.

JUST KIDDING. You better believe I sent it! This isn't that whole "write a letter and get rid of it but feel better anyway" situation. That might work well for some people, but the older I get, the more I realize that if we don't properly acknowledge our feelings—especially the tough ones—they will weigh us down. It is okay if hard things need to be said. I don't want to hide from that anymore. I don't want to hide from my tough emotions anymore, but instead feel them and express them as a simple step forward in moving *past* them.

A few hours after I hit send on the email, I got a response back from the medical assistant asking to meet at the mall food court for a fistfight that afternoon.

Not really, though a trip to the food court for any reason is probably a positive thing. But I did get a response from someone at the office, thanking me for reaching out, apologizing lightly, and telling me they were passing the note along to the assistant. And that was that. No mall fight required.

I felt so much better after sending the email. I didn't even need a response from her—heck I was surprised I even heard anything back at all. I just needed to express the thing that really hurt me and try to help the assistant not to do it to other parents.

And guess what. After I sent the email, I never thought of her face while punching things again, and it felt great. Now, I thought of more normal things, like how much I hated the mountain of laundry in my home that I could never seem to fully get to the bottom of. If anyone knows the answer to this, please email me.

I think sometimes in life it is okay to write letters that are not all sunshine and sparkles. To simply be honest with the people who have hurt you. It doesn't have to be dramatic, but it might have to be said plainly. It might not change much of anything, depending on the circumstance and the person receiving it especially. But if it fixes your spirit, even just a little, it might be worth it. Yes, forgiveness and grace are so important. As believers in Jesus, we are called to forgive like Jesus forgives us. And I don't know about you, but he is having to forgive me about, oh, every five minutes, on a good day. We all need grace. But that doesn't mean we have to ignore stuff that needs to be addressed. One time Jesus flipped over tables in a temple like he was in a holy episode of *Real Housewives*, so yeah. Righteous anger and all that.

Now, maybe it isn't a random medical assistant but perhaps a relative or an old friend who you need to write that letter to. Maybe it's . . . God. It is okay. I have been there too. I have asked him the hard questions about the painful things in my life and flat-out told him I was mad at how things were, and I do believe he can handle it. I do think he would rather hear of your hurt than not hear from you at all. If you need an example of this, read the Psalms or the book of Job. King David and Job lament something fierce, and they straight up ask God, *Um . . . why bro? Why does it have to be this way?* We have permission to do that too.

If God is the one you need to write the letter to, I hope you will. I hope you will pray with honesty as much as you need to. And I hope that heals something in your heart, and in your relationship with him, in the process.

You are so loved, and your feelings matter. So if someone or something has squashed your feelings like they were nothing more than a crusty cockroach crawling across the kitchen floor, I hope you will be kind to yourself and express that if it might help you. It might be what is needed to fully close the hurt and move forward stronger. Sometimes you need to offload some hurt you didn't ask for in the first place so you can stand a bit taller and be able to focus on hitting the things that actually deserve the energy. The things that you actually need to stand strong and face. Not just the things that are taking up emotional space in your life, uninvited.

So long, unwanted guests in our brains and hearts. Peace out, adieu, see ya never. May God fill that space with his peace instead, as we continue to walk forward with forgiveness, grace, and the occasional strongly worded letter.

CHAPTER FOURTEEN

Don't hate your neck for the next fifty years.

Oh Zoom, the bane of our existence. But also oddly convenient and I kinda like it? I don't know—do we love it or hate it? It is really hard to say. The pandemic made everything so confusing.

But anyway. One day, I was Zooming away on a work call with an author client, publisher, and a PR manager at my company, and I was playing the role of fun-yet-feisty publicist who definitely *will* tell you if the article you write for me to place is awful, sing your praises if you knock one out of the park, and forever pretend to love your book cover if there is no longer an option to change it.

All four of us were women in a different decade of life. From me in my thirties, to them in their fifties, sixties, and seventies. All four of us were accomplished, smart, and fierce ladies with a passion for writing, books, and telling stories that matter. A dream team of power, passion, and prose, slaying our careers and unneeded adjectives, and taking names along the way. Whew, I made that really dramatic. The point is, everyone on the Zoom call was awesome, a baddie, and crushing it—during our meeting and beyond. Strong women supporting strong women. Slap it on a T-shirt.

We were talking about books and media and TV appearances and all of the fun things that a book PR campaign entails, like how the author's book was influencing others and making a difference in the world, and what messages we wanted to highlight that would make the most impact. Then the author, the oldest of us, suddenly looked at her image on the Zoom screen and said, "Oh gosh—I hate my neck," and she pulled her turtleneck up a bit higher toward her chin. And with that, it set off a chain reaction of us all saying negative things about our appearances. The woman in her sixties quickly said, "Oh me too," and covered hers, and the woman in her fifties put both hands over her neck like she was going to strangle herself to death and agreed that she, too, hated her neck.

Then there was me, a lady in her midthirties. Not a total fresh spring chicken—I am far removed from the crop-top life of Gen Z—but I wasn't even considered in my "midlife" yet. AND GUESS WHAT? I, too, had recently started hating my neck. Shamefully, I admitted it on the Zoom call as well, for honesty, politeness, and solidarity's sake. Sigh.

So there we were, representing almost every decade of a woman's life—thirties to seventies—and we collectively agreed that we hated our *necks*. Of all the things to hate! Who taught us this?

As I sat there with these three brilliant, inspiring, successful women all covering their throats and making cutting comments about themselves that were so not deserved, I thought, *Do I really have fifty more years of simply hating the way that I look—neck, belly, thighs, and beyond?* That sounded exhausting and not very fun. There has to be a better way, right? I refuse to just succumb to more and more negative self-talk and thinking the older I get.

So, on that Zoom, as I was trying to politely laugh off all the self-deprecating comments and make work-approved pleasantries about it all, I silently vowed to be kinder to myself. To not just spend decade after decade hating every new sign of aging that inevitably will come. I refuse to just cave in to the cultural norm of hating my appearance as I get older, whatever that looks like for me, and whatever that looks like for you, if you want to join me. (Please do.) And while it is easy to say that on paper to sound super inspirational, it is something I am working through. It isn't easy, but I think working through it is better than nothing, right?

Over the past two years, I have gained some weight. It is enough to negatively affect my health, both mentally and physically, and guess what—I don't love it. It all came from mistreating myself and my body during a stressful time, and I am not proud of feeling anything positive about that. I am not trying to be a certain size or shape, but I am trying to feel good about myself and how I treat myself. For a while I wasn't doing that and it compounded. That is all. I guess I can partly blame Covid and quarantine of course, which brought about an incessant need to numb feelings and decompress with red wine and microwave popcorn post–kids' bedtime. This, turns out, becomes a very addictive habit to break, even when the world is "back to normal"—because there is always some excuse or some stressor, pandemic related or not.

Why am I telling you this? Because it isn't about weight gain, I have realized. I'm talking about this because even when I was at what I would now consider my "goal weight," or whatever, I *still* didn't love my body. Even when I was in college, pre–kid birthing and still doing ballet regularly, I thought a lot of the same negative thoughts about my body that I do now. I still looked at this part that wiggled with annoyance, poked at my small chin, and sighed over my thighs that have always been and forever will be #thicc. And now, with more weight and jiggle to account for, I think the same negative thoughts. This is ridiculous. When does this cycle stop? If I lose the weight, if I successfully keep my neck skin from flapping slightly in the wind, if I Botox my forehead into *Frozen* Elsa status—will that bring about happiness and contentment over my body? No. Because I have been younger and thinner, and I was still wishing I were . . . younger and thinner then, just like I am now.

It is clear to me now that true contentment over your looks and your body comes from someplace much deeper than the top of a scale with numbers you approve of. Even if I lost weight and did nothing to change how I treated my body, cared for my body, and cared for my mind, I would still feel negative about it unless I changed something internally. Because aging is something that we all have to walk through. Something nobody can stop or prevent. So, like other not-so-great things, we walk through it. What we can change is our perspective and attitude. Because it isn't about not placing your peace and happiness solely in a pair of size six jeans. It is about leveling up to simply treating yourself well, taking care of your body long-term.

I don't want to be the seventy-year-old on Zoom who is continuing the decades-long tradition of being a female who hates the soft skin on her neck.[1] Heck, I don't even want to be the forty-year-old lamenting about the dimples on her thighs. Or

[1] Or when I'm seventy, will we communicate via hologram chat? Who knows what the future holds, but surely we will progress past Zoom and cheesy greenscreen backgrounds.

the softness of her belly that one time held an entire human being inside of it. Or any of the totally natural and normal things that will forever just be a part of who we are. Because if we love ourselves well and without shame, are we not gently giving permission to someone else to do the same? I think we all need that.

There are ways we can care for ourselves better, of course. But I don't think we will ever finally feel like we're doing it all perfectly. We are humans, after all. What I do know is that I feel so much better when I exercise, don't drink stupid wine, don't eat gluten, and begin my days with Scripture, writing, and fresh air in my lungs. I know that, and I know that the space I function best in is where my mind is clear enough to fully enjoy this life. For my heart to feel proud of the way that I am treating myself. These are practical, simple ways to be healthy physically and emotionally. It isn't anything new, yet so often these good things can be pushed to the side, and we suffer in the process. So, I will keep striving to do more of the things that make me feel wholly well, and less of the things that ultimately detract from the true goodness in life. And I hope as you also strive to care for yourself well, you will really learn to love yourself well, no matter what size you are or how your chin looks in a photo. This is what I am working toward, somehow, someway. And it feels good.

We've all been through so much since the pandemic began. It will never not seem wild to me that all of us ... meaning the entire world ... collectively went through a big, awful challenge all at the same time. The details slightly varied, but it was all crap. We have *all* gone through so much, and have stood and fought to be strong in the face of all of it, because we simply had to. And that means something. So, can we just be kind to ourselves as we pick up the emotional and physical pieces? Care for ourselves gently, whatever that looks like individually? Can we vow to stop worrying about our necks and instead celebrate just how awesome we all are in our own unique ways?

We can take the energy wasted on negative thoughts and talk, and instead spend it by focusing on the beauty we are pouring into the world through our callings, our talents, and the love we are pouring into others. We can take the energy wasted on criticizing every photo taken of ourselves, and instead find one thing we do like and one thing we loved about that moment that we felt compelled to snap a pic. The beautiful weather that day, the way your child was laughing, the new outfit you had on that made you feel good, or simply wanting to remember the time you were spending with the ones you loved most.

Let's be a soft place for ourselves to land and learn to love ourselves a bit more, gobble necks and all. I will keep working on it, because it is something that takes time and practice. Join me if you want? And when I see you on Zoom, I am going to tell you how your neck is looking stellar, and mean it, queen.

PART 5

Ghosts, messy T-shirts, and chickens, because all these things totally make sense together.

HAVE YOU EVER THOUGHT ABOUT the divine connection between ghosts, messy T-shirts, and chickens?

You haven't? That is strange. Well, let's dig in here then.

The next chapters discuss things like poltergeists and poultry—but also important things like continuing to work on becoming stronger and better tackling the tough things in life. Also, the importance of community as we walk through whatever we are walking through. Being more open and honest with the people around us about the not-so-great times, and working to support and lift up our own flock of people who we encounter regularly. Sometimes for me, life lessons come through very strange, seemingly random places.

If you have read this far, you know that. Maybe this section can serve as a reminder to keep our eyes and hearts open for whatever God is trying to teach us. I hope that it will remind you of the beautiful things in life, even if they show up when you least expect them. Beauty through chickens, through vulnerability, and through continuing to fight for the life that you want.

CHAPTER FIFTEEN

Fire your ghost butler.

I need to fire my ghost butler. He doesn't do his job. See, all my adult life I at some level have been subconsciously expecting someone to swoop in and do the gross, boring, hard things for me. This "ghost butler"—dare we name him Jeeves?—is supposed to do my dishes, pick up my laundry, schedule doctors' appointments, exercise on my behalf but still give me the caloric deficit benefits, cook me healthy meals, and balance my budget. But it hasn't happened! Gall darn it, as they say in the Midwest. I think that this might be because . . . the stupid ghost doesn't exist. Boo. Pun might have been intended, you decide.

This reality is even scarier than an actual ghost—it's just us out here, folks, having to do the hard stuff all on our own. Lame! Well, the Lord does help get us through. But when was the last time Jesus Christ himself loaded your dishwasher? Exactly. That is on us.

It can be a difficult process to fully come to terms with the realization you are the only one who is going to do the hard, yucky things you are required to do. Or maybe it just is for me, an adult with ADHD who is on a perpetually hyperfocused quest to better herself in one way or the other.

I am talking about everything from picking up your dirty clothes off the floor to scheduling medical appointments to remembering to also take care of yourself during the really hard times so you don't completely fall apart—it can all feel like a lot, right? Just caring for yourself well during all the chaos can be the hardest part, truthfully. It is far easier to focus your energy on caring for others—a child, a spouse, the ten chickens you suddenly own—than yourself at times, for whatever reason.

But if we don't do these things—because as previously stated, the ghost that you thought would follow you around and clean up your chaos doesn't exist—the things will eventually get, well, messy. Physically, emotionally, spiritually—in all the ways, a big hot pile of mess. A mess hall. Messy bessy. Mess-bo-peep. However you want to label it, it isn't cute.

There is a point when you really need to face the music of life, even the kind that isn't fun to listen to, and accept you must walk through the hard thing step by step if you want the good outcomes. Nobody will walk through it on your behalf. I know that might sound a bit depressing. But it is also empowering. Because if you can stop trying to pass things off and make excuses, and realize how much of a baddie you are, and that you *can* do the hard stuff expected of you and get better at it and get used to it, then hey, how good would that feel?

For me, I got really tired of feeling like I was falling apart. I got tired of being a big mound of sadness, feeling blah and unhealthy, and having my home feel like it was one dirty dish away from combusting under the weight of the disorder. There are of course seasons where you have to give yourself grace. When you have tiny kids or a particularly crazy work schedule or are caring for a sick child, sometimes some of the things get put off for a bit. And it's okay. What isn't okay is when you are given the chance to put your feet firmly on the ground again and do something to care for yourself well, and you don't. That is where things get a bit prickly. Because if you are not happy with where things are at, you can take steps to make things better. Even if they are tiny steps.

There was a time when Kyle said, "Hey—we are in our midthirties. We either get better at this thing called life, or we get worse. We can either make our health and home a priority, or we don't. We can get better about cleaning up more and drinking less and parenting better and really putting in the time with the Lord. Or we can . . . get messier, sloppier, and sick." Kyle and I came to a place where we felt that for our family, for ourselves, we had to put the work in and do the good things.

What this looks like is working on being healthy physically, for myself and my family. It means finding a therapist, even though it's expensive and annoying, because I *know* it is needed during a really hard time. It means being on hold with the hospital for a long time but not letting it bug me anymore, because just accepting and expecting some things to suck and not caring is actually a boss move, and we need MORE BOSS MOVES in our arsenal, always. It's about taking the time to start my day with the Lord and worshiping and reading the Bible, and savoring how good that feels. Exercising and eating food that will nourish me, not wipe me out. It's spending less evenings drinking tequila and more days going on long walks with my best friend. It's going all in on swimming with my kids, goggles on, full-on mermaid mode, and having tea parties at the bottom of the pool with them. It is about showing up fully for this life, as best I can, little by little.

I need to take care of myself. So do you. Because nobody else is going to do it, dang it. Of course, God can work through us and with us, and help us grow in ways that we couldn't ever do on our own accord. We have that support, but we also need to take responsible steps in the right direction.

There is no invisible ghost who will take care of all our junk. But it's okay because we can do the hard things we need to do with God helping us along if we ask him. Especially when we are going through a season where our hearts, minds, and souls are pouring out into others—parenting, caring for a loved one who has a sickness, working at a demanding job—we simply have to do this. We have to cling to the Lord. We have to tell our nonexistent butler to get lost—we know they are never showing up anyway. We need to do the hard things with the Lord right there with us helping us along the way. Because if I know one thing, it is that every time I have tried to improve on my own—to just "do better, be better"—I have failed. I know I need the divine help of God to get me to a new, better place, and I know that help is freely given if we ask. I can't get there all on my own. So if we lean into that and level up, I do believe God will see us through, and strengthen us beyond the ways we could have ever done on our own

We spend so much time telling our kids to get more sleep, eat healthier foods and less sugar, drink more water, and be kind. We teach them to keep their rooms picked up, do their homework on time—do all the good things that don't always seem very fun but are so important for their overall wellness. Should we not do that for ourselves too? *So Katie—don't skip your workout. Don't skip your time with the Lord in the morning. Turn off the murder podcast and turn on some worship music, for goodness' sake! Give your brain something peaceful to marinate in, not just chaos. Be your own parent, because when you are a full-blown adult, nobody else is going to do it for you. And that is okay, because you can handle it, with God's grace.* We can grow and thrive and evolve into stronger, healthier versions of ourselves, especially if we ask the Lord to step in and help us where we keep falling short.

I hope you can gently, peacefully do even the tiniest amount of work for yourself that you do for your children, your spouse, your boss—even your pet pigs.[1] Start caring for yourself a little bit more and see what happens. Give yourself the grace that not only you give your loved ones, but that God gives us all the time—*his* children. It is easy to lose sight of that.

Listen, it isn't ever going to go perfectly. Likely, you may still ignore the laundry on the floor for an entire month during a busy season, or have a meltdown when things feel too hard one day and then eat an entire vegan cheesecake. But I hope you will remember how loved you are. I hope you remember how much you have done and do for others, and then do just a little bit for yourself too. Parent yourself in a kind, gentle way. See how it feels. And with that, don't ever lose sight of the radical, no-holds-back, never-ceasing love God gives us, no matter if we feel like we are crushing life or it is crushing us. Because it will always waver between the two.

I do know this. I do know that we can get stronger. There is still hope for you, for me, for us. We can continue to work toward being better, sturdier, more consistent, no matter how much we have messed up in the past. And I think we can rest

----

[1]My pet pigs are everything to me. Love you, Potato and Pumpkin, you little squishy, strange-looking balls of chunk.

in God's love as we take those steps, little by little, as he gives us a tiny bit of strength to take the next step forward. Then the next, a bit stronger. Because he is the one who can take us further than we could ever go on our own, grace by grace by grace.

CHAPTER SIXTEEN

Put your mess on a T-shirt and wear it proudly.

Do you ever think about the difference between the version of yourself most people see—online or even in person—and then what you are like behind closed doors? In your most non-Instagrammable moments? Oh, just me? You are a perfect little angel to your family who never loses their temper or does something dumb? Dang it, I knew it. I knew I was the only one who screwed up all the time.

It feels that way though sometimes, right? We present ourselves in life, and on social media especially, as our best—our literal life highlights reels. Which is fine and understandable! We all want to share our best sides and our best moments, and I think we mostly realize by this point to take everything with a filtered grain of salt. But when we share our best to a point where it makes other people feel like they are falling short, behind, or they are the only one that "doesn't have it all together," are we really doing a service to the world? Absolutely not.

If I'm following someone on social media, and their feed looks like a magazine spread I know I will never come close to achieving, I now just unfollow them. Or I hide them from my feed if we are friends in real life and I don't want them to *know*

I unfollowed them—that can get awkward. The older I get, the less patience I have for people who are pretending like they have it all figured out, for whatever reason that may be. I have wasted enough minutes of my life already feeling jealous of others. That is so 2009, the whole jealousy thing. Let's just launch that emotion into space with Elon Musk next time he makes the trip.

At some of my worst moments—during a full-on panic attack, in the middle of a spousal argument, being a big saddie in my bed and hiding from the world—I think about social media. What if, at that raw, tough moment, I decided to snap an alarmingly not-cute picture and post it online? Or what if when I had snot running down my nose from sobbing after a particularly hard day of parenting, I decided to go live and tell the world I had no good advice to give and I am just as wonky as the next person and am trying to just make it through? What would happen? Would people be weirded out, and then say, "Ooooh boy, at least I am not as messed up as Katie is"? Maybe a few holier-than-thou types, but that is fine. They have their own issues they might want to think through. I feel most would be like, "Wow—I have been there. I have felt that and said that and did that, but thought I was the only one." I would bet most people would simply relate, even if they didn't actually say so out loud.

I know when I've seen very vulnerable posts or read very honest books about the not-so-pretty parts of life, that is exactly how I felt. I felt seen and affirmed, assured we are all just doing our best here, each and every day, whatever that looks like. Nobody has it all together as we so falsely imagine. There are better times and harder times, but we are all just simply doing our best and trying to figure it all out as we go along.

Both sides of this spectrum make life up as a whole, right? It isn't *all* just about the doom, gloom, and destruction happening—cynicism can get old fast. I am all about being honest, but not all about being a negative Nancy.[1] Life really does have beautiful, sweet, near-perfect moments, and it is important we keep our eyes and hearts open to fully soak them in. Like when you hear a tiny baby give a belly laugh—there is no better sound in the world. Or the moment you realize you are way, way in love and have found your person forever. Or just cracking up with close friends late into the evening around champagne glasses that keep getting refilled. Or reaching a goal or a dream you have worked so hard for. Simply worshiping God and feeling his love so fully on a normal Thursday morning. There are good, seemingly perfect parts of life, and it's important to remember and share those times with others because the good things should be celebrated.

But there are also the tough parts, whichhhhh I know we are all aware of. Sometimes, the bad likes to stick around for a hot minute. Maybe even compound a bit and really test your strength and faith—boo, hiss, but fine we will lean into it. If you are reading this and feeling like you're more on the bad side than the good lately, I want you to know you are not alone. I have been there, everyone has been there, and many are there right now, even if they are hiding it behind a stream of perfectly curated pictures with matching tones. Everyone else around you doesn't have some secret magic trick to make their life glittery and perfect. Some people are just better at hiding their ugly from the rest of us.

---

[1]No relation to my amazing mom, Nancy, who is normally quite optimistic. Hi mom!

I had a moment once where this was so clearly spelled out for me. A friend texted our group chat that she felt like everyone else had it all together better than she did. She was sure everyone else around her was better at parenting, being a good spouse, keeping her home in order—all the things the world places so much pressure on. She felt like she was just constantly falling short and was far behind the other people she saw walking through similar seasons.

Have we not all felt that way?

And just as I was reading her texts about this, my room was still echoing from the sound of the door Kyle slammed as he stormed out of the room. We had a nothing fight, just a pointless moment where both of our stress levels got too high and we took our frustrations out on each other—the person we love the most in the world. The people we care for the deepest are often the ones who see the yuckiest side of us. It is crazy! Also beautiful, I suppose, that they see the roughest side of you and still stick around.

Anyway, I was sitting on my bedroom floor next to a pile of dirty laundry that I am pretty sure to this day still has not been folded. I was quietly crying, feeling sad, overwhelmed, and stuck when *bzz*. Her little text came in. Her little text saying everyone else—me included—had it all figured out and was mastering life way better than her. Oh lady, if you only knew.

Hey. To my friend and to you, listen up. You are not behind. You are not failing. We are all just living through this life the best we can, the best we know how with our given circumstances. Striving to not let each wave of stress and setbacks knock us down, at least not for too long. We all are trying to dust ourselves off, stand up, and try again. To float on top of the waves of life as they come. Because they will come, dang it. But the secret is to realize that and adapt. Not waste energy on trying to avoid the waves, hide from them, or pretend they don't exist, but fighting to ride on top of them, through the up and the down. I think mastering that—not letting the waves and setbacks of daily life throw you off, steal your joy, or surprise you—might be just about as close to having it "all figured out" as we can be.

There will be times when we feel like we are firmly on a glittery inflatable raft, sipping an ice-cold LaCroix, and calmly riding on top of whatever comes along. But there may be other times when we fall off into the water and are pummeled by the waves, time and again. It's okay. The important part is you work and fight to get back on, to get yourself stable and firmly floating again, so you can better handle what is next.

If we only ever present ourselves to others as living a life constantly on a flamingo floaty with a cocktail in hand and perfect hair unbothered by humidity and sweat, then we might make the people who are still in the waves feel even more like they are drowning.

So often we look at everyone else and their social highlight reels, and we don't really understand we are all a bit messy behind the scenes. For ourselves, yes, it is important to remember everyone has their low moments, and to avoid the lies of comparison as much as physically possible. But also, it is so important to be honest with others about your own struggles so you don't *contribute* to this perpetual, overarching lie that there are two categories in life: having it all figured out, and not. The lines between those two realms are so blurred, and it is important to normalize that so we can all navigate it a bit better and support each other along the way.

We would all benefit if we would be more upfront about the messy parts. Maybe we could even spell out our mess on a T-shirt, for everyone to see, so we all feel less alone about our own messes.[2] We could be open about the tough stuff, just as easily as we post that gorgeous pic on Instagram where our legs look nice. It might just be a tiny, powerful way we can all make this world a better place, by sharing the true human experience as best as possible. And in doing so, we can remind others they are not behind, failing, or just really bad at doing this thing called life. It is just, well, life itself. A sea of waves, good and bad, up and down. And we can choose to focus on the good and the beautiful—of course! But we can also encourage each other when times are anything but that.

We all have a bit of mess inside of us no photo filter can buff out. Not even those weird catfishing filters that make you look fifteen years younger can fully hide our grime. But it's okay! Maybe the grimy parts of life can be considered beautiful, in their own way, if we stop hiding them.

Yes, there is so much beauty in this life, which is so so so important to remember. It is far too easy to lose sight of the beauty if we just focus on the mess for too long. We must keep our eyes up and fixed on hope as best as we can. But I think being more open about the mess, about the grace and for- giveness and radical love it takes for us to even be a semi-okay,

---

[2]My T-shirt would say, "I have anxiety, depression, ADHD, I am ter- rible at cleaning, and I get overwhelmed by sounds every evening when I cook dinner for my family." But like, in a cute font and color palette, obviously.

functioning human being, just might be one of the most beau-tiful things we can do anyway. A mess yet beautiful. We are ALL a mess yet beautiful, and so, so loved by God.

I am a mess yet loved anyway.

I think I might actually make a T-shirt saying that. Please Venmo me twenty dollars if you would like one, you little messy beautiful loved beast you.

CHAPTER SEVENTEEN

Act like a chicken for the sake of humanity.

In January of 2021, I got chickens. I know—most people got puppies during the pandemic, but we were all set in the dog area with our trusty ten-year-old rescue who barks at anyone with a pulse for a solid eight minutes straight before attacking that person with love and kisses and tail wags. We had recently moved to our new home, which came equipped with 1.25 acres and an old, dilapidated chicken coop. So, one day Kyle went to the feed store and came home with six of the cutest little tiny fluff balls that cheeped. They cost $3.99 each, and I will never get over how inexpensive these pets are. I love me a good deal, even on living creatures.

I had never owned chickens. Eaten, clearly yes. But owned them when they were still alive? No way. Birds freaked me out! They are descendants of dinosaurs, a fact Shepherd reminds me of all the time. They even have a tiny knife on their face that they can peck you to death with if they want to. But apparently now I was the proud mother to six fluffy death dinos, and there was no turning back.

When Kyle was at the feed store picking them out, he decided to get one of each different breed. There was a chart showing you what they looked like as babies—mostly like cotton balls of slightly varying colors on two legs—and then what they looked like as adults, which was vastly different one from the next, with different feather colors and textures and strange tufts on their heads or sleek necks like a regal, royal chicken. The chart also showed how they all laid different colored eggs, which is fun and adds a bit to the intrigue and excitement. Who knew chickens had such variety!

We put a little brooder on our back porch, which basically means we set up a crib for chirping chicken babies to live life in until they were big enough to live elsewhere. Every day after work and when the kids would come home from school, we would go out there and play with our six little ladies, who were oddly friendly and had different personalities. Another chicken surprise! They have personalities! We all quickly fell in love. Once, Sunny put them on her lap and covered them with her dress and they sat there like she was their mama hen protecting them, and it was hilarious. To this day it's one of my favorite memories of Sunny, us both laughing so hard with six cheeping chickens sitting in her lap, cozying into her as if she gave birth to them herself. It was so cute.

Despite the little cheeping balls of joy and fluff living on my back porch, January 2021 was a really hard month for the nation. The insurrection happened, which was, well, horrifying and made me feel oddly vulnerable, like the world truly was falling apart and in disorder. There was a change in political office, and high tensions between parties. There were demonstrations and protests and just so much division. It felt heavy, with each and every new headline that blooped up on our phone screens or flashed on the television. Would the world ever stop feeling like this? Like we were one big, never-ending, messy argument about race, politics, masks, and vaccines with no clear resolve in sight?

Do you remember that feeling? Of complete helplessness as the nation seemed to swirl around you in anger, confusion, rage-induced awkward Facebook arguments, and just sadness? It felt like there was nothing we could do to ever get things back to a stable place, to raise our children or just exist happily. Peace felt so far from our grasp, and so far out of our control and from regaining it.

During these times, when things were mostly still quarantined or shut down, we had a lot of family dinners together—my sister, mom, dad, brother-in-law, niece, and nephew. We didn't see many other people except each other, once things felt safe to do so. We would just come together, watch the kids play, try to avoid any hard political talk, and enjoy life a bit. Remind one another of the blessings we all still had, no matter what was happening in the world.

During one of these family-dinner-party evenings, my sister and I were on my back porch as Sunny and my niece played with the baby chicks. Between their squeals of delight and laughter and their adorable mothering instincts they were giving the babies, our hearts were warmed up and thawed out just in the tiny way that we needed.

While we were still back there, my sister, Jenny, got quiet for a second, and then said:

"I know this is kinda cheesy, but there is something so inspiring about how these chicks are all completely different from one another but work together like one big happy family unit."

I had been thinking the same cheesy-yet-so-true thing. These little chickens all came from different backgrounds, were different breeds, and were one day going to lay totally different eggs. They even cheeped differently! But what they did was stick together, fiercely and instinctually. They were working together as *one* unit, united despite their differences for the common good of them all—the whole dang flock. Granted, their "common good" mostly involved getting as much food as possible and to at all times avoid being eaten by a hawk, but those are both noble quests. Sometimes, they even grouped together to keep each other warm, or cheeped really loudly when the food was arriving for the morning so the others would be aware and could run out and get their share. Or squawk a warning squawk when my cat was getting a little too close to the flock for their comfort.[1]

One unit, united together for the good of them *all*, despite them all being very different, looking different, and coming from different places and parts of the world.

And at that moment, the most inspiring example I could see displaying that was these baby chickens. Because man, 2020 had been a *year*. Never in my life had the nation felt more divided, leerier of each other, ready to pounce and on edge. I think most people thought with the magic tick of the clock at midnight on New Year's Eve, 2021 would be a lot better. But soon we all saw it wasn't going to be the case, and I think that made people even less hopeful than they already were. We realized the issues facing our country were sticking around a bit longer, and we had a lot more work to do.

It can be hard feeling so divided. Division in our country across parties and races, all the way down to our very own

---

[1] The cat never harms the chickens, all you PETA people. A hawk and my neighbor's renegade dog, on the other hand, sure did. RIP Elvis and Penguin.

families and friend groups. And Lord, have mercy, our stupid Facebook feeds that for some reason we keep going back to, despite them being a mostly constant stream of strife and horrors. I have seen firsthand hurtful things said and done within my own little circles, simply because people felt and believed different things, which apparently isn't allowed these days. Because we were different, in whatever way, shape, or form that took, and that was magnified by the events of 2020. And then 2021 and, well, 2022 also.

I know on a wide scale, the world will always be broken, separated, and divided to a degree. I think that is a part of sin, evil, and human nature. Darn. But I think what we can do, as an individual if nothing else, is our part by fighting back against that, even if in tiny form. Whoever is in your life, your circle, your human-being flock, work together with them no matter what your or their politics, religion, or beliefs are. Continue to love and listen and open your heart and mind up to opinions and thoughts of others that might not be the same as yours, without getting angry, having terrible family fights around the dinner table, or writing people off for good.

Next time you see how much hurt division causes, can you remember my cute tiny baby chicks? Can you remember that they were ones on this planet who were so different, yet remained so united, because it just *worked better that way.*[2] I think being united in kindness, in empathy, and with an open mind, despite differences, is only going to make the world feel a little bit brighter. And Lord knows we need the world to feel a bit brighter, these days especially. We all need each other, we need

----

[2]I know that is a slight exaggeration. Or an egg-zaggeration. But I am trying to make a point here.

to work together in unity and love and think about the others around us, no matter where they come from, what they look like, what they believe. No matter what their cheeps sound like, or the color of their eggs, or how wild their feathers are.

So yes, in January of 2021 baby chickens were the most inspiring thing I saw, which is very indicative of what the previous year had entailed. But I think as we continue on, we will still see more division, injustice, violence, and hurt. Sucks, right? I wish it weren't that way. But the generations before us and before them all had their own set of issues. At some point it's clear that it's a recurring part of human history. What we can do is focus on what we can control. We can work hard to build up our little flock around us.

What does this mean? Loving people fiercely, no matter what their beliefs are, what they look like, or their differences. Friending people who are outside of your norm and listening to them and their stories before making any assumptions or judgments.

Encourage the people who you encounter on the day to day. Support people, love people unconditionally, no matter how different they look from you. And yell really loud when food is getting brought out because maybe we all just need a snack. Snacks solve a lot of problems that at the time seem very serious.

Recognize the people you encounter regularly—coworkers, friends, family, neighbors, people you constantly run into at the grocery store, whoever is in your daily circle. And then fight for the common good of all of them, of the whole flock, as best you can. Take some advice from my baby chicks. Especially the one we named Edna because she really seems to know what's up.

Maybe if we all worked together better, no matter what your political, religious, and insert-whatever-divisive-word-here is, like a flock of little strange baby chickens, the world would be a better place. Perhaps next time someone posts a hurtful comment, or says something to slight you, just send the gift of baby chicks instead.[3]

Let's all return to the natural way of chickens: united, helping one another, and snuggling when it gets too cold out. Maybe that is our own human natural way as well. Needing one another, working together, no matter what you look like, what color your egg is, or what the sound of your cheep cheep cheep is.

Also, this just shows how strange the 2020s decade has become: seeing beauty and wisdom through tiny piles of feathers on toothpick legs. Lord, help us all. Cluck.

---

[3]I just want you to know that chickens can be purchased online and mailed anywhere around the country. Don't ask me how or why, but it is just another strange benefit of live poultry. But please don't actually do this.

PART 6

I would rather things be easy.

A QUESTION FOR YOU, and for God: Can we just *not* with the hard stuff, and just skip to the good parts of life? I think we all know that isn't possible. Yet do we not still yearn for that? Or is that just me—always wanting the easy road, despite history showing me the easy road is rarely open for business?

Even though our little human brains want things to be easy and without strife, we also know that they won't be, and despite that it will be okay. We can overcome the hard parts even though a nice nap instead sounds better.

This section will talk about a few times that made me scrunch my face up like the Grinch on his worst day and say, "but . . . can we not?" But of course, we must. We must walk through the hard times and fight to find joy and solid ground, even when things end up turning out the opposite of what we had planned for ourselves.

CHAPTER EIGHTEEN

Ride the waves, even in the rain.

One of my oldest friends, Kate, her husband, Nick, and their two adorable little girls were supposed to come to Florida for a week-long family vacation, and I was so excited. They deserved it—it had been a long hard year of parenting two small children, and then the frigid winter of Minnesota. I love sharing my state's sunshine with those who are vitamin-D deprived. Come visit—we will drink from coconuts, find shells in the sand, and get slightly sunburned. Heck—maybe we'll even swim with a manatee if we are lucky. The winter will soon be nothing but a cruel, distant memory as you are paddling along next to a big blob of gray squishiness bigger than a Toyota, feeding him lettuce and scratching his back rolls under the waves.[1]

I had been anticipating Kate coming for weeks, but as the date neared we realized, welp, it wasn't going to happen. Because she was supposed to arrive at the end of March 2020. The Wild West of the pandemic at its peak.

---

[1] This doesn't really happen with manatees, to be clear. You can swim near them but not feed and scratch them. Once I swam a little too close to one, and I got yelled at by a concerned passerby: "DO NOT PURSUE THE MANATEE." But like, lady, what if he *wants* to be pursued? Don't we all want to be pursued, just a little?

Naturally, Kate and her family had to cancel their trip. Her four-year-old was devastated, so I mailed them some kinetic sand as a weak attempt to re-create the beach in her Minnesota basement. And then, we all settled in to ride out whatever this whole pandemic situation was going to bring.

Eventually, things Covid-wise calmed down, a bit. They were actually able to rebook their flight down for the following October, which, in my opinion, is the best time to be in Florida anyway. At that time, the beaches were back open. Things had relatively settled down, for the moment at least. A lull between raging variants. We were looking forward to coming back together and enjoying some sunshine, virus-free sea air, and as much relaxation as possible with four small children between us, which isn't much. But ya gotta at least try!

The first day Kate and her family arrived in the Sunshine State, it rained. Not like a ferocious fifteen-minute-long afternoon storm Floridians are so used to getting that we sometimes won't even leave the beach for it because we know it will pass. Nah. This was more of a wet, thick gray blanket of drizzle and drops. Like a Minnesota winter but warmer and more humid so your hair was frizzier.

We were happy to be together anyway and said, "Hey—the sun will probably come out tomorrow. The weather changes so quickly here, we will get our beach time."

How foolishly optimistic we were. The rain never let up. Day after day, the entire. time. they. were. on. their. family. vacation. it. rained.

After all the drama of canceling the first time, rescheduling and booking, and having high hopes for a bit of respite in the middle of a very stressful few months, it just . . . rained. And I was mad. I was mad on their behalf. I was mad for all of us, who had grand plans to enjoy the warm weather and sun and try for a few days to pretend that the world was normal and not a dumpster fire of chaos.

At what point does all the rain stop and the clouds part? That has to come, right? The year prior felt like enough penance paid. We all went through enough stress and strife to earn at least one fun weekend on vacation, right? But we all know that is not how life works.

A few days in, when we were sure we were going to have bad weather the entire week, I asked Kate if she was upset. I mean she had every right to be! I was upset *for* her. But, in her cheery demeanor, she just laughed and said "What do you expect? It's 2020!"

And I loved that. I loved that she knew in a really hard year how to adjust her expectations and standards. Not to allow whatever crap thing that was happening to have more power than it deserved and interfere with her day-to-day happiness. She could have come to Florida, been sad she would be leaving paler than when she arrived, gone home frustrated, and then waited to see what the next blow 2020 would bring with frustration.

Instead she realized, hey—this year was tough. Who is to say a vacation would magically fix all that mess, anyway? There are good times and there are hard ones, and yes sometimes the hard ones last a *bit* longer than we would have liked or expected. But it is so important to simply try and make the best out of whatever circumstance you are facing. Because the alternative isn't all that great.

And guess what. Despite the rain, we still had a really fun time together. It wasn't exactly how we had planned it would turn out in the first place, but with adjusting our expectations a bit, we still had a good week.

That trip with my friend, her good attitude and ability to bring her own sunshine to the rainy Florida gloom, I realized something. Maybe it isn't just 2020, the pandemic, whatever crazy world event is happening, that's the cause of all this crappy stuff. Maybe it's, well, just *life*. Maybe this world is broken and can be oh so hard, global crisis or not.

I saw somewhere once after big, negative occurrences, like pandemics or personal tragedies, any little negative thing that happens becomes just another reason to throw your hands up in the air and be like, "Oh great. Another awful thing has happened—just add it to the list! I must be cursed. The moon must be in retrograde, and I must be finally getting my karma payback for that time I stained my sister's sweater and hid it from her."

But I worry we might get stuck in that mindset, for good. During the pandemic, what used to be just the normal bumps and bruises of life felt far more elevated and upsetting. Some of it was justified, of course. Because it seems like ever since Covid, it has been a string of one bad thing to one bad thing to one bad thing, all chained together by new variants going around and getting our families sick. AGAIN. Even beyond the virus, if you watch the news, it seems each and every day is another tragedy that brings more fear, anxiety, and heartache to our lives. Lord Jesus, how much more can we take?

Yes, times were and are at this moment definitely more challenging than in some other seasons of history—I'm looking at you, nineties, when the economy was great, kids were able to run outside freely, and everyone was just enjoying their new microwave. Now I am sometimes paying five dollars for a gallon of gas, and sometimes my phone alerts me when I may have been exposed to Covid, and I don't understand how it knows that.

Despite that, I am working hard to see past the pattern of never-ending doom the pandemic has brought about. I'm trying to go back to the more neutral mindset of, *Hey—maybe this is just life, right?* Maybe it always has been a bit rocky, but pre-2020 we had a bit more strength, emotional energy, and grit left in us to stand up and fight back against it. Maybe life isn't just one big compounded pile of crap as it feels like these days, but just contains a few natural bumps along the way as we all work to do our best.

Because, as I said, it isn't just 2020. It isn't just 2021, or 2022, or 2023, or 2024 that is out to get us. It is life. It can be hard and broken but also so precious and beautiful. And we can lose sight of that side of the equation. For example, the summer of 2020 we were confined to my backyard with nothing but a little kiddie pool and two toddlers. But sweet, precious, simple family memories were made as we all crowded in that pool, lit the back porch twinkle lights, played the Bob Marley, and pretended like we were at the beach and it wasn't actually closed. Our family slowed down and really enjoyed time with just the four of us. It was hard but sweet at the same time. And I am really, really trying to keep my eye on the sweet these days.

So yes, it rained on my friend's vacation. How rude of the world to do that to her! But the months of quarantine leading up to our time together were able to give her the perspective that even though it was wet and gloomy, we were still together. And heck—at least we had that after months of isolation. We were having fun. The kids were running wild in the house, fueled with joy from just being with their friends. It didn't bother them it was raining—all they saw were endless opportunities for play and adventure. Us adults were able to sit and talk for at least a few minutes without being asked for a glass of water, a butt wipe, or a snack, which for me is a little vacation in itself. We all kept laughing and catching up and resting, enjoying our little bit of time together as best we could. And, despite the rain, it was sweet, and it was enough.

This isn't meant to be discouraging. I am not saying, "Oh, just expect the world to always suck, and learn to deal with it." Because sometimes it won't suck—sometimes it can and will blow you away by the good times, the beauty, the ease. But consider the source, right? Life has always been a bit rocky at times. The pandemic amplified that by a lot. It has also always been beautiful and a gift, virus swirling around or not. So we can just search for that side of the coin. The good side. The side that shows us no matter what comes our way, we can work to enjoy the days that we have been blessed with, rain or shine.

Perhaps pandemics, long drawn-out hardships, never-ending medical issues, or loneliness that continues far longer than we would like might be a crash course in how to form resilience and perspective so we can better enjoy the days ahead, which very well may be brighter. Super hard things can and do make us stronger, so then the easy times are even easier. A lot of rain can teach us to dance, no matter what the weather, and see the beauty even between the clouds.

CHAPTER NINETEEN

....

Sometimes life throws you a plot twist.

We had a major life plot twist. I had scheduled a virtual appointment with Shepherd's neurosurgeon just to touch base, which we have done about every six months or so since he was born. She had me walk through how Shepherd was doing, and truthfully, I did have a few concerns. But it was so hard to know if they were a real issue, or just him being three. So I told her what I noticed. I told her it is usually hard for him to walk even short distances. He got tired very easily, and we ended up having to carry him, far more than I ever remembered having to do for my daughter. He would randomly complain of leg pain that just didn't seem like growing pains, and a few other concerning things. It was all so hard—a continual gray area of wondering. Was he exhibiting normal three-year-old behavior, or was his spinal cord definitely tethered and starting to cause symptoms?

When I told Shepherd's neurosurgeon all this, she said those are 100 percent symptoms of having a tethered spinal cord and he needed surgery. I think somewhere in my heart I expected she would say that. Kyle and I had already discussed this possibility, that she would say it was time for surgery. We decided we would wait until next summer, when he was a bit older and a bit more aware. A three-year-old understanding why he was confined to a hospital bed and in pain just felt really difficult. So—I told her, maybe next summer, at the ripe-old-age of almost five, we would do the surgery.

Andddd she straight up said NOPE. We needed to do it now—as soon as we could, actually. This woman—one of the very few female pediatric neurosurgeons in the country, and a mother of four herself—had been so patient with us throughout our very long journey of figuring out my sweet dude's special body over the past three years. She had been kind and empathetic to us as very horrified parents trying to navigate what the absolute next best step for our son was. She was always gentle, always open to our questions and hesitations about just diving straight into surgery. But now, her foot was down. She could tell it was time. No more waiting and watching. The symptoms Shepherd was displaying were textbook and indicative his spinal cord was in distress, and it could lead toward permanent nerve damage. Even paralysis if left untreated, so yeah, it was time.

And it was time for Kyle and me to face the fear that had been taking up so much of our headspace since Shepherd was born. Until now, by the grace of God, we had been able to avoid any surgeries. The scariest thing we had faced was having him go under full anesthesia for a sedated MRI, which was traumatic in its own right. But now, we were going all in. We would be checking in to the hospital that was already so familiar to us, and I could already imagine saying to registration that we were there for neurosurgery, and what that would feel like in my heart.

Kyle and I would now be the parents we would see shuffling around in their pajamas as they stood in the long line at the

Starbucks on the first floor looking beyond exhausted. We would be the ones wheeling our little child in a wheelchair just to get him a breath of fresh air. We were going to have to face the very hard, scary thing, head on.

When we ended the Teladoc appointment, I tried to hold it together okay as the reality of our situation began to sink in. Okay, this summer. The plan was now *this summer*. Maybe in a month or two even—surely there had to be a long wait for a surgery like this. Something so big and serious and, well, surgery-y. Anything we had to schedule for Shepherd up to this point always was pushed so far out, giving us weeks to emotionally prepare, grieve, stress over, pray about, and then finally come to terms with the procedure. Now, when I called the scheduling department and explained what we needed to do, the woman didn't suggest a few months away, a few weeks even. She said, "How about this Tuesday?"

And that was when I fell apart.

I mean who does she think I am? An emotional processing Sonic the Hedgehog? Tuesday is too soon, Tuesday feels impossible. I began to cry on the phone, which is always so awkward, but she was so kind. I am sure she is pretty dang used to talking with crying moms at this point since she schedules neuro-surgeries for children. Together, we decided on three weeks out. That felt like just long enough to get ready emotionally and physically, without pushing it too far out to cause Shepherd any harm.

So, that was that. The surgery was planned. In three weeks we would have to do the hardest thing of our life to date.

Of course, now every brain cell I had was consumed with my son. Despite that, life still had to keep going on. Oddly enough,

I had to finish up this book, which was due one week after surgery. It seemed so weird to me that I had spent the five months prior writing about walking through very difficult things that you do NOT want to walk through, and now here I was, about to fight the Nintendo Boss of all the hard things. So, I had to ask myself, *Even now, as you are walking through one of the darkest, scariest seasons you have ever faced—can you still stand behind what you wrote?*

And I realized the answer was yes.

Also, I quickly asked for a one-month extension on when my first draft was due because I am not a superhero, and there was no way I was going to be able to focus on finishing a book strong and on the literal life of my precious child at the same time. Duh. Also, I wanted to see what I felt like on the other side of the "big hard thing." Surely, I would learn something, right?

In the first week after scheduling the surgery I felt okay, I guess, considering. I attribute this to the people that immediately began praying for us. Their prayers kept us upright in a very upside-down time. But sometimes, when I knew the anxiety was creeping in that day or the sadness felt extra thick when I opened my eyes in the morning, I had to make myself a list. Usually my list making would help me in typical anxiety-ridden situations like packing or moving or anything big and monumental where I wrote out every task I had to do. But now, my list was smaller, scaled back, but so important nonetheless. Usually it would be

1. Wake up

2. Get dressed

3. Coffee

4. Workout

5. Read the Bible

6. Shower

7. Start work

I had to literally remind myself to start my day in a way that filled me up and to give myself a very practical path to do so. To simply survive and function, I had to create as strong a foundation as possible to stand on that day and carry me through. Otherwise I was sure to crumble, like an old forgotten cookie that fell beneath the grocery store bakery counter.

Did I *feel* like exercising, reading the amazing Word of God, and having a lovely warm shower? Not a chance. I wanted to put my hair in a ponytail, avoid any ounce of makeup, and then just roll my way into the chaos of life and flail around until I could hide in my bed again. But I knew I had to force myself to do the things that were good for me. Just like we force our own kids to do things that are good for them— eating vegetables, general hygiene, going to bed at a decent hour so they don't wake up like a screaming banshee the next day. Sometimes we need to parent ourselves, and do those things for ourselves, if we are going to survive. So I tried to do that, as best I could.

The first week and then the next, I asked for a lot of prayer from a lot of people, I made my little beyond-simple lists, and I did the tiny things that kept me *mostly* okay emotionally, all sometimes broken up by a few hours of hiding under a comforter, processing big feelings, and numbing out on TikTok while I quietly wept over what I knew was to come for my child. Weeping and scrolling and hiding were mostly all I could muster as I attempted to process what was to come. Kyle, on the other hand, poured his anxiety into stress cleaning—I wish that is what I did! But instead I made lists and tried to not cry for as long as possible and we, well, we fumbled along okay.

Then we hit the one-week-out mark. Now, in my mind, I was saying over and over, *Next week. Next week is the week my son is having surgery on his spinal cord. It is next week.*

Something about the surgery being just a few days away broke me down. I knew it was so close to being game time. We were really going to be doing this, and I *knew* it was going to be so hard. On us as parents, yes. But mostly on my son, which of course is what wrecks us as parents in the first place. That is what this all is about—him having to suffer and it breaking your heart. You're the one who is supposed to take the hits, take the pain, make it all better, but I knew I wasn't going to be able to. We would do everything in our power to make it go as smoothly as possible, but I knew Kyle and I wouldn't be able to *fully* comfort him, cheer him up, or stop his tears as he was forced to lie flat on his back for twenty-four hours post-surgery, to relearn how to sit up and go to the bathroom, or to try and walk again. To just deal with the pain.

I didn't want Shepherd to have to go through it all. I didn't want to have to go through it, I didn't want Kyle to have to do it. But dang, we had to do it anyway. So buckle up, baby.

As we approached the day of the surgery, I emotionally felt stripped bare and raw, like an old, tear-stained mattress tossed aside in an alley. Nothing—no workout, words from a friend, reading Scripture, or *anything*—was enough for me to stop feeling the very large, scary emotions I was feeling. None of my tips and tricks, my lists and distractions, could help me avoid the very real grief and fear. I felt my bucket was completely empty and dry, and I was just sad.

But also, there at the bottom of that rusty, not-cute bucket was one thing. One thing remained, constant and keeping me on solid ground, as best I could be.

It was Jesus.

And if that cheesy Sunday school answer feels cheap to you, sorry bro. But there is no denying it was the grace of Jesus that kept me upright and breathing when I felt I was at my very darkest and very worst. Have you ever been in a place like that? A very, very hard place where your normal comforts, your normal answers, vices, and distractions are taken from you, and you are left there to just exist in the middle of something really awful? It's not pretty.

I felt stripped of everything, but I still had Jesus. I still had the Lord, and he was enough to inflate my heart just enough to keep it beating normally. He was there, he was holding me up and holding me together, more than anything else could, and I was so grateful. Did I like being at the bottom of my bucket? Heck no. Did I feel a deep, lasting sense of comfort knowing God was there and would always be there no matter what awful, crappy, not fun thing happened in my life? Absolutely. Clearly feeling him there, in my hardest, worst moments, reminded me he has been and will be there all along. That will never, ever change.

I do believe that God will be at the bottom of your empty buckets too, even though I so wish you would never ever have to go there to find him. I do think he will always be there for you to give a little light in the darkest of times. To help you stand up straight and keep walking forward. To comfort you in a time where comfort feels impossible.

The weekend before the surgery, I knew we had to get out of the house and do something fun as a family. I had seen the previous weekend's pattern. If I didn't exit our home quick enough, I would eventually find myself back in bed crying while Kyle stress organized a cupboard in our kitchen, both of us taking turns having emotional outbursts at each other that were clearly misplaced stress. I couldn't fall into that again, so I gathered up the troops and we headed on a little family adventure.

We decided to go north to a beach I had heard about called Blowing Rocks. Most of South Florida's beaches are just flat and simple—gorgeous, but no big rocks or cliffs like California or Hawaii. But in our county, there was this one little area where there *were* rocky cliffs for some reason. And, when the tide hits them just right, the water sprays up into the air dramatically like that one part in *The Little Mermaid* where Ariel props herself up on a rock with the sea spraying everywhere behind her.[1]

We drove the forty minutes north to Blowing Rocks with hopes of seeing, well, rocks that blew out water and stuff. I don't know, I was a mess, okay? When we got there, the tide was low, so it was less splashy drama but more of a fun natural playground of rocks we could climb on and explore. The short cliffs were full of caves, pockets, and discarded seashells, and the kids loved it. We started to walk along the seashore, looking at the dried barnacles or creatures the tide had left behind. We walked, and walked, and in our excitement suddenly realized we walked

---

[1] Every girl born in the nineties and beyond has tried to re-create this moment at least once in her lifetime.

pretty dang far and would now have to walk back. So we began, but both kids started to whine and slow down, and Kyle and I were also carrying all of our shoes and were ourselves kinda worn out from the heat, waves, and wind. You know—how almost all fun outings with kids end . . . in chaos.

We kept pushing forward and telling the kids it wasn't much farther. Eventually, we could finally see the little path that would take us back to the car. But at that moment, Shepherd had had enough. He sat in the sand and began to cry and would not get up. He said his legs hurt and he couldn't walk any farther. He was at the bottom of his own bucket in that moment. And what did he have there? Kyle and me, to carry him forward. He couldn't walk any farther, but we could carry him to where he needed to go.

On the beach, as I watched Kyle scoop Shepherd up and hold him close, I knew that is what God would do for me during the final stretch of really hard stuff too. I knew he would also pick me up and walk me forward when I felt I simply didn't have the strength to keep going forward.

Remember the poem "Footprints in the Sand" that was printed on posters and put on basically every church office wall in the nineties? If you didn't grow up in old-school evangelical popular culture, this is the general premise: A man had a dream, and he saw two sets of footprints in the sand—one from him, one from God. But then there were places with only one set of footprints, during his hardest times. Crushed, he says to God, "I don't understand why when I needed you most you would leave me." And God said, "During your times of trial and suffering, when you see only one set of footprints, it was then that I carried you."

Never in my wildest 1997-youth-group dreams would I imagine I would seriously be referencing that poem in a book, but here we are.

We were literally, in this moment, living that out. Carrying our son across the sand when he was having a hard time. And God was carrying us at the same time.

With the surgery just days away, I felt it was physically impossible to take another step forward. I felt I simply did not have it in me. Then there was God, who was holding me close and walking on my behalf. Keeping me moving forward. Being my strength when I didn't feel like I could be my own, just like we would do for Shepherd in the hospital and as he recovered.

The next few days were a blur. Suddenly, it was the night before the surgery and we were dropping Sunny off at my sister's, not really knowing when all four of us would be together again or how long we would be staying in the hospital. The next morning we placed a sleeping Shepherd in the car at five o'clock for our two-hour drive to Miami. I was running on prayers, caffeine, and my body's miraculous ability to pump out a ton of adrenaline and rise up to function in the face of something very, very scary.

We did okay in the pre-op portion. Shep was in a good mood despite being in a hospital gown and not being able to eat or drink anything the entire morning. Eventually, the nurses came to wheel him away. I told Shepherd—who at that point was sedated on something they called "happy juice," which made him act like a twenty-one-year-old on their first night out at a bar—to tell them all about the new Jurassic Park movie, and he did. He was happily discussing Mosasauruses and blue raptors as he left our sight. Our baby was now in the complete care of someone else—his literal life and well-being in the hands of others, and Kyle and I were just left standing there alone. It was surreal.

We went to the crowded waiting room, and just, well, continued to breathe oxygen and exist. We passed the time by staring into space, texting our people a quick update that it had all started, and then staring into space some more. That was about all we could muster. Then two hours in, I got a call and a nurse told me the anesthesia process and prep work were done, and they were beginning actual surgery. It was then I started bawling, which is kinda awkward in a crowded waiting room, but we were all there for the same awful reason anyway, so someone had to be the awkward-loud-crying one from time to time. I let it out—the feels, the emotions—let them rise up and pour out. I felt them as strongly as I could, hoping they would pass quickly so I could be ready to care for my child when he was finally brought back to us.

Two more hours passed, and we got another call—it was done and it went perfectly. They let me go back to see Shepherd in post-op—one parent allowed only, so I walked back alone. Shepherd was still sleeping with a ton of wires and machines hooked on him, but he was okay. He was *okay*, and it felt like I took my first breath of the day.

What followed were five days of living on the neurosurgery recovery floor, just caring for Shepherd's every need around the clock. Lying with him in the bed for two full days and nights because he wasn't able to sit up yet. Making sure the nurses stayed on top of his pain meds. Trying to keep him happy and eating. Encouraging him to do simple things like pee, then sit up in the bed, then even take a few steps with us holding him up. Day by day, moment by moment, Kyle and I just helped him get back on his feet, to be as comfortable as possible, and to do the next brave thing needed to recover.

The last night we were there, he was doing so much better. He was in good spirits but getting restless and bored, which I think is a good sign. I asked the nurse if we could take him out in a wheelchair, and we took him all over the hospital, getting popsicles and visiting the free book library, and then outside for his first breath of fresh air in days. It really perked us all up—a small feeling of joy and normalcy after a long, stressful week.

We wheeled him back up in the room and he stayed in the chair so he could finish his popsicle. As we were all just sitting there, he suddenly said, "Do you like my dance moves?" and did the silliest wheelchair-bound dance moves possible, with a huge grin on his face. They were, of course, the best dance moves I had *ever* seen, and in that moment I knew we were going to be okay.

We went home the next day, and almost instantly Shepherd relaxed and began to take huge strides forward. He began walking mostly normally, was happily playing with his toys, and loved showing his sister his "scratch" on his back and then checking out the healing process himself in the mirror.

Kyle and I worked on decompressing from the trauma we just went through. And I fully mean trauma. Yes, we had the best outcome possible and were so grateful, but sometimes you need a hot minute to get your feet back on the ground. Our church brought us so many meals, and day by day Shepherd got better and better, and we rested and reset and just chilled out. We felt like we were getting our footing again and back into our groove as a family.

The week after Shepherd's surgery, when we started seeing family and friends again, everyone said the same thing: he is standing taller. It was like the release of his spinal cord let him stand firm and fully upright as he was always meant to do. And he stopped asking us to carry him. Even just one week out of a very major surgery, he was walking stronger and better than he ever had before. When we went back to the hospital for his two-week post-surgery appointment, he ran through the halls, and I cried a few happy tears. He had never made it through that massive hospital before without a stroller or us carrying him, and now he was laughing and running like any other wild three-year-old boy, and it was the most beautiful thing.

Shepherd had to go through a really hard thing, and as parents we walked right through it with him, carrying the emotional weight of it that he didn't fully understand as a three-year-old. But he came out on the other side stronger, better, and more fully himself. He is now able to run and thrive in a way I didn't even know was possible for him.

Sometimes we also have to go through hard times so we can emerge on the other side stronger.

Would I have given anything to prevent my child from having to go through surgery? Of course. But Shepherd had to do it. And I wonder if God knew *I* had to—for some reason I am not even sure of yet as this all is so freshly unfolding—walk through the really hard thing also. The literal effects for me are not as physically apparent as Shep's straight back and ability to run laps around the backyard like a superhero.

But I can say now, after having walked through one of the hardest things I have ever had to go through, there are two things I know for sure. First, God was there at the lowest, darkest point when I felt I couldn't walk another step. And, if I ever get that low again, he will still be there. He will be there if I collapse and feel like I can't keep going. He will be the one who scoops me out of the sand and keeps me moving forward. And, of course, he will do just the same for you too.

Psalm 23, made popular by Coolio's *Gangsta's Paradise* (I am kidding haha), is so beloved for a reason. It is worth including it here, for either new eyes or ones who need the reminder—because I sure need it, again and again.

> The LORD is my shepherd, I lack nothing.
>   He makes me lie down in green pastures,
> he leads me beside quiet waters,
>   he refreshes my soul.
> He guides me along the right paths
>   for his name's sake.
> Even though I walk
>   through the darkest valley,
> I will fear no evil,
>   for you are with me;
> your rod and your staff,
>   they comfort me.
>
> You prepare a table before me
>   in the presence of my enemies.
> You anoint my head with oil;
>   my cup overflows.
> Surely your goodness and love will follow me
>   all the days of my life,
> and I will dwell in the house of the LORD
>   forever.

This psalm doesn't explain why we are walking through the dark valley. God doesn't even pluck us right out of the dark valley and onto a sunny mountaintop, darn it. We have to walk through, for reasons unknown. But this is the beautiful thing: What we do know is he is right there, guiding us every step of the way. Strengthening us. Comforting us. Protecting us. Even feeding us, thank goodness.

In my darkest moment, I felt the Lord so clearly. And I know, whatever happens in the future, he will be right there, just as he was before, is now, and always will be. His goodness and love will follow me all the days of my life. And yours too.

Conclusion

W e may not ever know why hard things happen on this side of heaven. Sometimes, you can see why things work out in a certain way, which is nice. It might hurt at first, but eventually you gain the perspective that it all really was for the best. But sometimes, you can't see a reason why things happen. And for me, understanding that frees something in me. We don't always know why the hard things, the bad things, happen. And that is okay. Accepting that we might not have an answer sometimes is enough to bring the closure you need in the first place.

I certainly don't have the answer as to why we have to walk through big, scary, tough things. By now you have also realized that I don't have the "five quick tips on how to not just survive but thrive!" type of guru-BS to share with you. Nah. We don't have full control over exactly how our lives will play out, and accepting that can be cathartic. It's important to admit that you are a bit powerless, and instead fully lean on the grace of God to help you through whatever it is you have to face. Maybe that is the strongest thing you can do. The one thing that won't fail you, no matter what.

Through our tough medical journey—that is still rolling right along—or the pandemic, or just the drudgery of everyday life, I can get to a point where I'm tired of feeling like I'm sinking beneath the weight of it all. I don't want to feel that way—so what the heck is the alternative? It's to simply expect the waves and try to ride them as best I can when they come. Keeping my head held high. Keeping my eyes fixed on God and his goodness, and the hope he provides. Hope that when I lean into it, it can feel like Christmas morning, but year-round and with less cookies involved and better weather. Having hope sometimes takes strength. Having hope sometimes takes courage. But having hope also feels a lot better than just floundering around and getting further and further underwater. So, well, *hope.*

I will keep fighting hard for hope. I will keep fighting hard for joy. I will keep throwing punches at the tough stuff and judo chopping it in the gullet as many times as necessary. I will keep reminding my brain of what is good and true. I will be so deeply kind to myself when I need a minute to process, grieve, and feel all the feels even when I don't want to. I hope you will too. Because the bad feelings will pass. Sunshine comes again. Joy comes again. I really do know that to be true.

This is all we can do. Keep fighting for the good stuff. Keep standing up and fixing our eyes on hope, on the beauty of this precious gift that is life. Keep creating moments of ridiculous dancing and laughter, even if stuck in a wheelchair while doing so or at ten in the evening when your kids are finally asleep and you have your first chance to breathe for the day.

What other option is there, right? We must look for and fight for and savor the good, even in the hard times. Because I do believe it is there, all along. In its time, it will show itself. We will find it, again and again.

You can do this, even when things are really hard. You—yes you—are stronger than you realize. And so is God. He is stronger than we realize. And he is right there with ya, no matter what.

<3 Katie

Acknowledgments

I would like to thank my agent, Rachel Kent, for all her guidance and valuable feedback that helped this book come to life. I am so grateful to work with you! Thank you to the team at InterVarsity Press for helping all my author dreams come true, again. To Al Hsu, for your amazing editorial feedback and funny notes in the comments that kept me laughing throughout my editing. Thank you to my church and all our friends there, for not only giving me so many good things to write about but also loving and supporting my family so well during the harder times with meals, prayers, and so much love. Thank you to my family, for all the love, support and listening ears that you have given during the past few wild years on our medical journey. And for your support of my author career. Thank you to Sunny and Shepherd, for showing me what resilience and true strength look like, and reminding me that joy and laughter can be found in every situation. Thank you to Kyle, for, well, all the things. For keeping me laughing during every season we walk through. For always, always believing I could be an author and giving me the time and space to write when it is needed. And for simply being you—the best dude and dad around.

About the Author

Katie Schnack is an author and a book publicist. Her first book, *The Gap Decade: When You're Technically an Adult but Really Don't Feel Like It* talks about that gray area of being a grownup but still really confused about what it means to be, well, a grownup. Katie has also been featured in *Relevant,* Today.com, Hello Giggles, Romper, and Scary Mommy. Katie and her family now live in West Palm Beach, Florida, on an acre of land with way too many animals to list here.

For more, visit katieschnack.com and follow her on Instagram (@katieschnack), Facebook (@katieschnackwriter), and TikTok (@katieschnack), where she will never participate in a dance trend.